SHURLEY ENGLISH

HOMESCHOOL MADE EASY

LEVEL 6

Student Book

By
Brenda Shurley

Shurley Instructional Materials, Inc., Cabot, Arkansas

04-14
Shurley English Homeschooling
Level 6 Student Workbook
ISBN 978-1-58561-029-7

Shurley
Instructional
Materials, Inc.

Printed in the United States of America by RR Donnelley, Owensville, MO.

For additional information or to place an order, write to: Shurley Instructional Materials, Inc.
366 SIM Drive
Cabot, AR 72023

1 2 3 4 5 6 7 8 9   14 13 11 09 07 05 04 03 01

JINGLE

SECTION

Jingle Section

Jingle 1: Noun Jingle

Yo! Ho! It's a NOUN we know!
A noun names a person,
A noun names a place,
A noun names a person, place, or thing,
And sometimes an idea!
Person, Place, Thing, Idea.

Finding nouns is a game.
Listen now to the nouns we name:
Head, shoulders, knees, and toes,
Girls, boys, shoes, and clothes.

Yo! Ho! It's a NOUN we know!
Yo! Ho! It's a NOUN we know!
Person, Place, Thing, Idea.
Person, Place, Thing, Idea.
Now it's time to say Yo! Whoa!

Jingle: Verb Jingle

A verb, a verb. What is a verb?
Haven't you heard?
There are two kinds of verbs:
The action verb and the linking verb.

The action verb shows a state of action,
Like **stand** and **sit** and **smile**.
The action verb is always doing
Because it tells what the subject does.
We **stand**! We **sit**! We **smile**!

The linking verb is a state of being,
Like **am, is, are, was**, and **were**,
Looks, becomes, grows, and **feels**.
A linking verb shows no action
Because it tells what the subject is.
He **is** *a clown.*
He **looks** *funny.*

Jingle 3: Sentence Jingle

A sentence, sentence, sentence
Is complete, complete, complete
When 5 simple rules
It meets, meets, meets.

It has a subject, subject, subject
And a verb, verb, verb.
It makes sense, sense, sense
With every word, word, word.

Add a capital letter, letter
And an end mark, mark.
Now, we're finished, and aren't we smart!
Now, our sentence has all its parts!

REMEMBER
Subject, Verb, Com-plete sense,
Capital letter, and an end mark, too.
That's what a sentence is all about!

Jingle Section

Jingle 4: Adverb Jingle

An adverb modifies a verb, adjective, or another adverb.
An adverb asks *How? When? Where?*
To find an adverb: **Go, Ask, Get**.
Where do I **go**? To a verb, adjective, or another adverb.
What do I **ask**? How? When? Where?
What do I **get**? An ADVERB! (Clap) (Clap)
That's what!

Jingle 5: Adjective Jingle

An adjective modifies a noun or pronoun.
An adjective asks *What kind? Which one? How many?*
To find an adjective: **Go, Ask, Get**.
Where do I **go**? To a noun or pronoun.
What do I **ask**? What kind? Which one? How many?
What do I **get**? An ADJECTIVE! (Clap) (Clap)
That's what!

Jingle 6: Article Adjective Jingle

We are the article adjectives,
Teeny, tiny adjectives:
A, AN, THE - A, AN, THE.

We are called article adjectives and noun markers;
We are memorized and used every day.
So, if you spot us, you can mark us
With the label A.

We are the article adjectives,
Teeny, tiny adjectives:
A, AN, THE - A, AN, THE.

Jingle 7: Preposition Jingle

A PREP PREP PREPOSITION
Is a special group of words
That connects a
NOUN, NOUN, NOUN
Or a PRO, PRO, PRONOUN
To the rest of the sentence.

Jingle 8: Object of the Prep Jingle

Dum De Dum Dum!
An O-P is a N-O-U-N or a P-R-O
After the P-R-E-P
In a S-E-N-T-E-N-C-E.
Dum De Dum Dum - DONE!

Jingle Section

Jingle 9: Preposition Flow Jingle		
1. **Preposition, Preposition Starting with an A.** (Fast) aboard, about, above, across, after, against, (Slow) along, among, around, at.	2. **Preposition, Preposition Starting with a B.** (Fast) before, behind, below, beneath, beside, between, (Slow) beyond, but, by.	3. **Preposition, Preposition Starting with a D.** down (slow & long), during (snappy).
4. **Preposition, Preposition Don't go away. Go to the middle And see what we say. E-F-I and L-N-O** except, for, from, in, inside, into, like, near, of, off, on, out, outside, over.	5. **Preposition, Preposition Almost through. Start with P and end with W.** past, since, through, throughout, to, toward, under, underneath, until, up, upon, with, within, without.	6. **Preposition, Preposition Easy as can be. We're all finished, And aren't you pleased? We've just recited All 49 of these.**

Jingle 10: Pronoun Jingle
These little pronouns, Hanging around, Takes the place of all the nouns. With a smile and a nod, And a twinkle of the eye,. Give those pronouns A big high-five! Yea!

Jingle 11: Subject Pronoun Jingle
There are seven subject pronouns That are easy as can be: I and we,   (clap 2 times) He and she,   (clap 2 times) It and they and you.   (clap 3 times)

Jingle 12: Possessive Pronoun Jingle
There are seven possessive pronouns That are easy as can be: My and our,   (clap 2 times) His and her,   (clap 2 times) Its and their and your.   (clap 3 times)

Jingle 13: Object Pronoun Jingle
There are seven object pronouns That are easy as can be: Me and us,   (clap 2 times) Him and her,   (clap 2 times) It and them and you.   (clap 3 times)

Jingle Section

Jingle 14: The 23 Helping Verbs of the Mean, Lean Verb Machine Jingle

These 23 helping verbs will be on my test.
I gotta remember them so I can do my best.
I'll start out with 8 and finish with 15;
Just call me the mean, lean verb machine.

There are 8 **be** verbs that are easy as can be:
am, is, are – was and were,
am, is, are – was and were,
am, is, are – was and were,
be, being, and been.

All together now, the 8 **be** verbs:
am, is, are – was and were – be, being, and been.
am, is, are – was and were – be, being, and been.

There're 23 helping verbs, and I've recited only 8.
That leaves fifteen more that I must relate:
has, have, and had – do, does, and did,
has, have, and had – do, does, and did,
might, must, may – might, must, may.

Knowing these verbs will save my grade:
can and could – would and should,
can and could – would and should,
shall and will,
shall and will.

In record time, I did this drill.
I'm the mean, lean verb machine - STILL!

Jingle 15: Eight Parts of Speech Jingle

Want to know how to write?
Use the eight parts of speech - They're dynamite!

Nouns, **V**erbs, and **P**ronouns - They rule!
They're called the **NVP's**, and they're really cool!
The **Double A's** are on the move;
Adjectives and **A**dverbs help you groove!
Next come the **PIC's**, and then we're done!
The **PIC's** are **P**reposition, **I**nterjection, and **C**onjunction!

All together now, the eight parts of speech, abbreviations please:
NVP, AA, PIC   NVP, AA, PIC!

Jingle 16: Direct Object Jingle

1. A direct object is a noun or pronoun.
2. A direct object completes the meaning of the of the sentence.
3. A direct object is located after the verb-transitive
4. To find the direct object, ask WHAT or WHOM after your verb.

Jingle 17: Indirect Object Jingle

1. An indirect object is a noun or pronoun.
2. An indirect object receives what the direct object names.
3. An indirect object is located between the verb-transitive and the direct object.
4. To find the indirect object, ask TO WHOM or FOR WHOM after the direct object.

Jingle Section

Jingle 18A: Predicate Noun Jingle

1. A predicate noun is a noun or pronoun.
2. A predicate noun means the same thing as the subject word.
3. A predicate noun is located after a linking verb.
4. To find the predicate noun, ask WHAT or WHO after the verb.

Jingle 18B: Another Predicate Noun Jingle

Listen, my comrades, and you shall hear
About predicate nouns from far and near.
No one knows the time or year
When the predicate nouns will appear.
Listen now to all the facts,
So you will know when the **Pred's** are back!

Dum De Dum Dum!
A **pred**icate noun is a special noun in the predicate
That means the same thing as the subject word.
To find a **pred**icate noun, ask *what* or *who*
After a linking verb.

Jingle 19A: Predicate Adjective Jingle

1. A predicate adjective is an adjective in the predicate.
2. A predicate adjective modifies only the subject word.
3. A predicate adjective is located after a linking verb.
4. To find the predicate adjective ask WHAT KIND of subject.

Jingle 19B: Another Predicate Adjective Jingle

Listen, my comrades, and you shall hear
About predicate adjectives from far and near.
No one knows the time or year
When the predicate adjectives will appear.
Listen now to all the facts,
So you will know when the **Pred's** are back!

Dum De Dum Dum!
A **pred**icate adjective is a special adjective in the predicate
That modifies only the subject word.
To find a **pred**icate adjective, ask *what kind of subject*
After a linking verb.

REFERENCE

SECTION

Vocabulary Reference

Chapter 1, Vocabulary Words #1	Chapter 1, Vocabulary Words #2
(defer, postpone, astute, obtuse)	(commodities, goods, disprove, attest)

Chapter 2, Vocabulary Words #1	Chapter 2, Vocabulary Words #2
(loquacious, garrulous, gargantuan, diminutive)	(germinate, stagnate, exuberant, flamboyant)

Chapter 3, Vocabulary Words #1	Chapter 3, Vocabulary Words #2
(endorse, denounce, bereavement, loss)	(predicament, dilemma, tribulation, ecstasy)

Chapter 4, Vocabulary Words #1	Chapter 4, Vocabulary Words #2
(obfuscate, confuse, deplorable, admirable)	(complicated, intricate, preposterous, reasonable)

Chapter 5, Vocabulary Words #1	Chapter 5, Vocabulary Words #2
(benevolent, charitable, methodical, chaotic)	(contingency, serendipity, frugal, extravagant)

Chapter 6, Vocabulary Words #1	Chapter 6, Vocabulary Words #2
(congenial, compatible, docile, aggressive)	(travail, labor, swoon, revive)

Chapter 7, Vocabulary Words #1	Chapter 7, Vocabulary Words #2
(felicitous, melancholy, entreat, beseech)	(obvious, ambiguous, sumptuous, lavish)

Chapter 8, Vocabulary Words #1	Chapter 8, Vocabulary Words #2
(collate, sort, ancestor, descendant)	(surmise, guess, terminate, initiate)

Chapter 9, Vocabulary Words #1	Chapter 9, Vocabulary Words #2
(superfluous, redundant, svelte, corpulent)	(compulsory, mandatory, neutral, partial)

Chapter 10, Vocabulary Words #1	Chapter 10, Vocabulary Words #2
(impulsive, impetuous, swelter, freeze)	(transient, permanent, building, edifice)

Chapter 11, Vocabulary Words #1	Chapter 11, Vocabulary Words #2
(meager, sparse, pleasurable, tedious)	(valor, courage, transform, preserve)

Chapter 12, Vocabulary Words #1	Chapter 12, Vocabulary Words #2
(integrity, honesty, tactful, undiplomatic)	(expedite, hurry, tawdry, elegant)

Chapter 13, Vocabulary Words #1	Chapter 13, Vocabulary Words #2
(confide, entrust, profuse, trifling)	(tranquil, turbulent, pallid, pale)

Chapter 14, Vocabulary Words #1	Chapter 14, Vocabulary Words #2
(defunct, extinct, frigid, torrid)	(discourteous, rude, triumph, succumb)

Chapter 15, Vocabulary Words #1	Chapter 15, Vocabulary Words #2
(terrestrial, aquatic, discreet, prudent)	(eccentric, odd, mutter, enunciate)

Vocabulary Reference

Chapter 16, Vocabulary Words #1	Chapter 16, Vocabulary Words #2
(ebullient, exhilarated, appease, antagonize)	(hapless, unlucky, futile, essential)

Chapter 17, Vocabulary Words #1	Chapter 17, Vocabulary Words #2
(herald, announce, constant, variable)	(impediment, obstacle, paraphrased, verbatim)

Chapter 18, Vocabulary Words #1	Chapter 18, Vocabulary Words #2
(impeccable, flawless, vindicate, indict)	(innocuous, harmless, voluntary, coerce)

Chapter 19, Vocabulary Words #1	Chapter 19, Vocabulary Words #2
(unappealing, winsome, free, liberate)	(ludicrous, ridiculous, sensitive, callous)

Chapter 20, Vocabulary Words #1	Chapter 20, Vocabulary Words #2
(malleable, pliable, brevity, longevity)	(manifold, numerous, brazen, decent)

Chapter 21, Vocabulary Words #1	Chapter 21, Vocabulary Words #2
(mendicant, beggar, predictable, capricious)	(monstrous, enormous, verbose, prolix)

Chapter 22, Vocabulary Words #1	Chapter 22, Vocabulary Words #2
(nebulous, vague, chastise, applaud)	(remiss, negligent, clarify, obscure)

Chapter 23, Vocabulary Words #1	Chapter 23, Vocabulary Words #2
(revolting, disgusting, comply, resist)	(oppressive, overbearing, disparate, uniform)

Chapter 24, Vocabulary Words #1	Chapter 24, Vocabulary Words #2
(paltry, insignificant, manageable, incorrigible)	(perjury, untruth, authentic, counterfeit)

Chapter 25, Vocabulary Words #1	Chapter 25, Vocabulary Words #2
(pilfer, steal, deify, vilify)	(pious, sacred, barbaric, civilized)

Chapter 26, Vocabulary Words #1	Chapter 26, Vocabulary Words #2
(requirement, option, recant, withdraw)	(intensify, placate, recline, repose)

Chapter 27, Vocabulary Words #1	Chapter 27, Vocabulary Words #2
(subvert, undermine, periodic, systematic)	(succinct, brief, obstreperous, rambunctious)

Chapter 28, Vocabulary Words #1	Chapter 28, Vocabulary Words #2
(serene, tranquil, prosperity, adversity)	(taint, contaminate, ameliorate, deteriorate)

Reference 1: Beginning Setup Plan for Homeschool

You should use this plan to keep things in order!

1. Have separate color-coded pocket folders for each subject.
2. Put unfinished work in the right-hand side and finished work in the left-hand side of each subject folder.
3. Put notes to study, graded tests, and study guides in the brads so you will have them to study for scheduled tests.
4. Have a paper folder to store extra clean sheets of paper. Keep it full at all times.
5. Have an assignment folder to be reviewed every day.

Things to keep in your assignment folder:

A. Keep a monthly calendar of assignments, test dates, report-due dates, project-due dates, extra activities, dates and times, review dates, etc.

B. Keep a grade sheet to record the grades received in each subject. (*You might also consider keeping your grades on the inside cover of each subject folder. However you keep your grades, just remember to keep up with them accurately. Your grades are your business, so keep up with them! Grades help you know which areas need attention.*)

C. Make a list every day of the things you want to do so you can keep track of what you finish and what you do not finish. Move the unfinished items to your new list the next day. (*Yes, making this list takes time, but it's your road map to success. You will always know at a glance what you set out to accomplish and what still needs to be done.*)

6. Keep all necessary school supplies in a handy, heavy-duty plastic bag or a pencil bag.

Reference 2: Synonyms, Antonyms, and Six-Step Vocabulary Plan

Part 1: Synonyms and Antonyms

Definitions: Synonyms are words that have similar or almost the same meanings. Antonyms are words that have opposite meanings.

Directions: Identify each pair of words as synonyms or antonyms by putting parentheses ( ) around *syn* or *ant*.

1. hasty, rapid **(syn)** ant   2. night, evening **(syn)** ant   3. kind, harsh syn **(ant)**

Part 2: Six-Step Vocabulary Plan

(1) Write a title for the vocabulary words in each chapter.
Example: **Chapter 1, Vocabulary Words #1**

(2) Write each vocabulary word in your vocabulary notebook.

(3) Look up each vocabulary word in a dictionary or thesaurus.

(4) Write the meaning beside each vocabulary word.

(5) Write a sentence that helps you remember how each vocabulary word is used.

(6) Write and identify a pair of synonym words and a pair of antonym words.

Reference 3: What is Journal Writing?

Journal Writing is a written record of your personal thoughts and feelings about things or people that are important to you. Recording your thoughts in a journal is a good way to remember how you felt about what was happening in your life at a particular time. You can record your dreams, memories, feelings, and experiences. You can ask questions and answer some of them. It is fun to go back later and read what you have written because it shows how you have changed in different areas of your life. A journal can also be an excellent place to look for future writing topics, creative stories, poems, etc. Writing in a journal is an easy and enjoyable way to practice your writing skills without worrying about a writing grade.

What do I write about?

Journals are personal, but sometimes it helps to have ideas to get you started. Remember, in a journal, you do not have to stick to one topic. Write about someone or something you like. Write about what you did last weekend or on vacation. Write about what you hope to do this week or on your next vacation. Write about home, school, friends, hobbies, special talents (yours or someone else's), present and future hopes and fears. Write about what is wrong in your world and what you would do to "fix" it. Write about the good things and the bad things in your world. If you think about a past event and want to write an opinion about it now, put it in your journal. If you want to give your opinion about a present or future event that could have an impact on your life or the way you see things, put it in your journal. If something bothers you, record it in your journal. If something interests you, record it. If you just want to record something that doesn't seem important at all, write it in your journal. After all, it is your journal!

How do I get started writing in my personal journal?

You need to put the day's date on the title line of your paper: **Month, Day, Year.** Skip the next line and begin your entry. You might write one or two sentences, a paragraph, a whole page, or several pages. Except for the journal date, no particular organizational style is required for journal writing. You decide how best to organize and express your thoughts. Feel free to include sketches, diagrams, lists, etc., if they will help you remember your thoughts about a topic or an event. You will also need a spiral notebook, a pen, a quiet place, and at least 5-10 minutes of uninterrupted writing time.

Note: Use a pen if possible. Pencils have lead points that break and erasers, both of which slow down your thoughts. Any drawings you might include do not have to be masterpieces—stick figures will do nicely.

Reference 4: Checklists

Revision Checklist

1. Eliminate unnecessary or needlessly repeated words or ideas.
2. Combine or reorder sentences.
3. Change word choices for clarity and expression.
4. Know the purpose: to explain, to describe, to entertain, or to persuade.
5. Know the audience: the reader(s) of the writing.

Beginning Editing Checklist

1. Did you indent the paragraph?
2. Did you capitalize the first word and put an end mark at the end of every sentence?
3. Did you spell words correctly?

More Editing Skills

4. Did you follow the writing guidelines? (*located in Reference 13 on student page 14*)
5. Did you list the topic and three points on separate lines at the top of the paper?
6. Did you follow the three-point paragraph pattern?
7. Did you write in the point of view assigned? (*first or third person*)
8. Did you use the correct homonyms?
9. Did you follow all other capitalization and punctuation rules?
10. Did you follow the three-paragraph essay pattern?

Final Paper Checklist

1. Have you written the correct heading on your paper?
2. Have you written your final paper in ink?
3. Have you single-spaced your final paper?
4. Have you written your final paper neatly?
5. Have you stapled the final paper to the rough draft and handed them in to your teacher?

Writing Process Checklist

1. Gather information.
2. Write a rough draft.
3. Revise the rough draft.
4. Edit the rough draft.
5. Write a final paper.

Reference 5:
Rough Draft

When Travis came home from work, last night, the fog was so thick that he couldnt hardly see. Travis pulled off the road twice, because he couldnt see the road. Travis got home an our later then he would normally get home. His hands were shaking, his voice was shaky too. When Travis hit the couch, he was out like a light. In the morning he promised himself that he would never drive home under those conditions again.

Revision of Draft

When Travis **returned** home from work, last night, the fog was so **dense** that he couldnt **barely** see. **Twice he pulled off the highway**, because he couldnt see **to drive**. **Finally he arrived home an hour later then usual**. His **hands and voice trembled from the trama of his drive-home**. **The minute he hit the couch** he was out like a light. **After a sound nights sleep he vowed never to drive home again under these conditions**.

Edit Draft

When Travis returned home from work [**delete comma**] last night, the fog was so dense that he could [*could, not couldnt*] barely see. Twice, [**comma inserted**] he pulled off the highway [**comma deleted**] because he couldn't [**apostrophe added**] see to drive. Finally, [**comma inserted**] he arrived home, [**comma inserted**] an hour later than [*than, not then*] usual. His hands and voice trembled from the trauma [*trauma, not trama*] of his drive home [**no hyphen**]. The minute he "hit the couch," [**figure of speech; add quotation marks and a comma**] he was "out like a light." [**figure of speech; add quotation marks**] After a sound night's [**apostrophe added**] sleep, [**comma inserted**]he vowed never to drive home again under these conditions.

Final Paragraph

When Travis returned home from work last night, the fog was so dense that he could barely see. Twice, he pulled off the highway because he couldn't see to drive. Finally, he arrived home, an hour later than usual. His hands and voice trembled from the trauma of his drive home. The minute he "hit the couch," he was "out like a light." After a sound night's sleep, he vowed never to drive home again under these conditions.

Reference 6: The Four Kinds of Sentences and the End Mark Flow	
1. A **declarative** sentence makes a statement. It is labeled with a **D**. Example: Larry played soccer yesterday. (Period, statement, declarative sentence)	3. An **interrogative** sentence asks a question. It is labeled with an **Int**. Example: Did you like the new movie? (Question mark, question, interrogative sentence)
2. An **imperative** sentence gives a command. It is labeled with an **Imp**. Example: Put your books on your desk. (Period, command, imperative sentence)	4. An **exclamatory** sentence expresses strong feeling. It is labeled with an **E**. Example: The barn is on fire! (Exclamation point, strong feeling, exclamatory sentence)

Examples: Read each sentence, recite the end-mark flow in parentheses, and put the end mark and the abbreviation for the sentence type in the blank at the end of each sentence.

1. Larry helped his brother **. D**
   (Period, statement, declarative sentence)

3. Put your equipment in the garage **. Imp**
   (Period, command, imperative sentence)

2. The lion ran toward me **! E**
   (Exclamation point, strong feeling, exclamatory sentence)

4. Are you going to the meeting **? Int**
   (Question mark, question, interrogative sentence)

Reference 7: Additional Article Adjective Information

1. *A/An* are called <u>indefinite</u> articles, meaning one of several.
   (Examples: **a** fly swatter—**an** answer.)

2. *The* is called a <u>definite</u> article, meaning the only one there is.
   (Examples: **the** fly swatter—**the** answer.)

3. The article *The* has two pronunciations:

   a. As a long **e** (*where the article precedes a word that begins with a vowel sound: the egg, the igloo*)

   b. As a short **u** (*where the article precedes a word that begins with a consonant sound: the dance, the shoe*)

Reference 8: Question and Answer Flow Sentence

Question and Answer Flow Sentence: The excited girls danced perfectly.

1. Who danced perfectly? girls - SN
2. What is being said about girls? girls danced - V
3. Danced how? perfectly - Adv
4. What kind of girls? excited - Adj
5. The - A

Classified Sentence:

A	Adj	SN	V	Adv
The	excited	girls	danced	perfectly.

Reference 9: Question and Answer Flow Sentence

Question and Answer Flow for Sentence 1: The delightful children performed splendidly.

1. Who performed splendidly? children - SN
2. What is being said about children? children performed - V
3. Performed how? splendidly - Adv
4. What kind of children? delightful - Adj
5. The - A

6. SN V P1 Check
   (*Say: Subject Noun, Verb, Pattern 1, Check.*)
7. Period, statement, declarative sentence
8. Go back to the verb - divide the complete subject from the complete predicate.

Classified Sentence:

<u>SN V</u>   A   Adj   SN   V   Adv
P1   The delightful children / performed splendidly. **D**

Reference 10: Definitions for a Skill Builder Check

1. A **noun** names a person, place, thing, or idea.

2. A **common noun** names ANY person, place, or thing. A common noun is not capitalized because it does not name a special person, place, or thing. (*boy, house*)

3. A **proper noun** is a noun that names a special, or particular, person, place, or thing. Proper nouns are always capitalized no matter where they are located in the sentence. (*Jan, Europe*)

4. A **singular noun** usually does not end in an *s* or *es* and means only one. Some nouns end in s and are singular and mean only one. (*cat, child, gas*)

5. A **plural noun** usually ends in an *s* or *es* and means more than one. Some nouns are made plural by changing their spelling. (*cats, children, gases*)

6. A **simple subject** is another name for the subject noun or subject pronoun.

7. A **simple predicate** is another name for the verb.

Reference 11: Noun Job Chart

Directions: Underline the complete subject once and the complete predicate twice in the sentence below. Then, complete the table below.

	A	Adj	SN	V	Adv	Adv

1. **SN V**   <u>The sweaty runners</u> / <u><u>limped slowly away</u></u>. D
   P1

List the Noun Used	List the Noun Job	Singular or Plural	Common or Proper	Simple Subject	Simple Predicate
runners	SN	P	C	runners	limped

Reference 12: Adverb Exception

From: (The young soldiers <u>swiftly</u> / *advanced*.) To show the adverb exception: (The young soldiers / <u>swiftly advanced</u>.)

To add the adverb exception to the Question and Answer Flow, say, "*Is there an adverb exception?*" If there is not an adverb before the verb you say, "*No.*" If there is an adverb before the verb, you say, "*Yes - change the line.*"

Reference 13: Writing Guidelines

1. Label your writing assignment in the top right-hand corner of your page with the following information:
   A. Your Name
   B. The Writing Assignment Number *(Example: WA#1, WA#2, etc.)*
   C. Type of Writing (Examples: Expository Paragraph, Persuasive Essay, Descriptive Paragraph, etc.)
   D. The title of the writing on the top of the first line

2. Think about the topic which you are assigned.

3. Think about the type of writing assigned, which is the purpose for the writing.
   (Is your writing intended to explain, persuade, describe, or narrate?)

4. Think about the writing format, which is the organizational plan you are expected to use.
   (Is your assignment a paragraph, a 3-paragraph essay, a 5-paragraph essay, or a letter?)

5. Use your writing time wisely.
   (Begin work quickly and concentrate on your assignment until it is finished.)

Reference 14: This reference is located on page 15.

Reference 15: Natural and Inverted Word Order

Introduction: A **Natural Order** sentence has all subject parts first and all predicate parts after the verb. **Inverted Order** means that a sentence has predicate words in the complete subject. When a word is located in the complete subject but modifies the verb, it is a predicate word in the complete subject. A sentence with inverted order has one of these predicate words at the beginning of the complete subject: **an adverb, a helping verb, or a prepositional phrase**.

1. An adverb at the beginning of the sentence will modify the verb.
   (Example: <u>Yesterday</u>, <u>we</u> / <u><u>went to the school play</u></u>.) (<u>We</u> / <u><u>went to the school play yesterday</u></u>.)

2. A helping verb at the beginning of a sentence will always be part of the verb.
   (Example: <u><u>Are</u></u> <u>you</u> / <u><u>going to the game</u></u>?) (<u>You</u> / <u><u>are going to the game</u></u>.)

3. A prepositional phrase at the beginning of a sentence will oftentimes modify the verb.
   (Example: <u>After the game</u>, <u>we</u> / <u><u>went home</u></u>.) (<u>We</u> / <u><u>went home after the game</u></u>.)

To add inverted order to the Question and Answer Flow, say, "*Is this sentence in a natural or inverted order?*" If there are no predicate words in the complete subject, you say, "*Natural - No change.*" If there are predicate words at the beginning of the complete subject, you say, "*Inverted - Underline the subject parts once and the predicate parts twice.*" To show the inverted order, draw one line under the subject parts and two lines under the predicate parts.

Reference 14: Three-Point Paragraph Example

Topic: **My favorite sports**

Three main points: 1. **football**   2. **ice skating**   3. **diving**

Sentence #1 – <u>Topic Sentence</u> (*Use words in the topic and tell how many points will be used.*)
I have three favorite sports.

Sentence #2 – <u>3-Point Sentence</u> (*List the 3 points in the order you will present them.*)
These sports are football, ice skating, and diving.

Sentence #3 – <u>First Point</u>
My first favorite sport is football.

Sentence #4 – <u>Supporting Sentence</u> for the first point.
I like football because it has cheering fans, cheerleaders, and a team of fighting players trying to score.

Sentence #5 – <u>Second Point</u>
My second favorite sport is ice skating.

Sentence #6 – <u>Supporting Sentence</u> for the second point.
I enjoy watching the exciting ice skaters do beautiful, and even dangerous, jumps that keep me on the edge of my seat.

Sentence #7 – <u>Third Point</u>
My third favorite sport is diving.

Sentence #8 – <u>Supporting Sentence</u> for the third point.
I love watching divers leap from high diving boards or high cliffs.

Sentence #9 – <u>Concluding (final) Sentence</u>. (*Restate the topic sentence and add an extra thought.*)
I could watch these three sports over and over because I love the excitement they produce.

SAMPLE PARAGRAPH

My Favorite Sports

I have three favorite sports. These sports are football, ice skating, and diving. My first favorite sport is football. I like football because it has cheering fans, cheerleaders, and a team of fighting players who are trying to score. My second favorite sport is ice skating. I enjoy watching the exciting ice skaters do beautiful, and even dangerous, jumps that keep me on the edge of my seat. My third favorite sport is diving. I love watching divers leap from high diving boards or high cliffs. I could watch these three sports over and over because I love the excitement they produce.

Reference 16: Practice Sentence						
Labels:	A	Adj	Adj	SN	V	Adv	Adv
Practice:	**An**	**angry**	**old**	**alligator**	**swam**	**forward**	**suddenly.**

Reference 17: Improved Sentence						
Labels:	**A**	**Adj**	**Adj**	**SN**	**V**	**Adv**	**Adv**
Practice:	An	angry	old	alligator	swam	forward	suddenly.
Improved:	**The**	**perturbed**	**ancient**	**crocodile**	**floated**	**away**	**disgustedly.**
	(word change)	(synonym)	(synonym)	(synonym)	(synonym)	(antonym)	(word change)

Reference 18: Subject-Verb Agreement Rules

Rule 1: A singular subject must use a singular verb form that ends in **s**: *is, was, has, does, or verbs ending with* **es**.
Rule 2: A plural subject, a compound subject, or the subject **YOU** must use a plural verb form that has **no s** ending: *are, were, do, have, or verbs without* **s** *or* **es** *endings*. (A plural verb form is also called the *plain form*.)

Examples: For each sentence, do these four things: (1) Write the subject. (2) Write **S** if the subject is singular or **P** if the subject is plural. (3) Write the rule number. (4) Underline the correct verb in the sentence.

Subject	S or P	Rule	
boy	S	1	1. The **boy** (jump, <u>jumps</u>) on his trampoline.
hat and coat	P	2	2. Your **hat** and **coat** (is, <u>are</u>) in the closet.
You	P	2	3. **You** (<u>help</u>, helps) with the chores.

Reference 19: Knowing the Difference Between Prepositions and Adverbs

                                Adv
In the sample sentence, *Chuck fell **down***, the word *down* is an adverb because it does not have a noun after it.

                        P   noun (**OP**)
In the sample sentence, *Chuck fell **down the stairs***, the word *down* is a preposition because it has the noun *stairs* (the object of the preposition) after it.

To find the preposition and object of the preposition in the Question and Answer Flow, say:

    down - P   (Say: *down - preposition*)
    down what? stairs - OP   (Say: *down what? stairs - object of the preposition*)

Reference 20: Writing in First Person or Third Person

Events and stories can be told from different viewpoints.

First Person Point of View uses the first person pronouns *I, we, me, us, my, our, mine,* and *ours* to name the speaker. If any of the first person pronouns are used in a writing, the writing is automatically considered a first person writing, even though second and third person pronouns may also be used. First person shows that you (the writer) are speaking, and that you (the writer) are personally involved in what is happening.

(<u>Examples</u>: **I** am going sledding on **my** new sled. He likes **my** sled.)

Third Person Point of View uses the third person pronouns *he, his, him, she, her, hers, it, its, they, their, theirs,* and *them* to name the person or thing spoken about. You may <u>not</u> use the first person pronouns *I, we, us, our, me, my, mine,* and *ours* because using any first person pronouns automatically puts a writing in a first person point of view. Third person means that you (the writer) must write as if you are watching the events take place. Third person shows that you are writing about another person, thing, or event.

(<u>Examples</u>: **He** is going sledding on **his** new sled. **She** likes **his** sled.)

Reference 21: Possessive Nouns

1. A possessive noun is the name of a person, place, or thing that owns something.
2. A possessive noun will always have an apostrophe after it. It will have either an *apostrophe* before the <u>s</u> (*'s*) or an *apostrophe* after the <u>s</u> (*s'*). The apostrophe makes a noun show ownership. (*Kim's car*)
3. A possessive noun has two jobs: to show ownership or possession and to modify like an adjective.
4. When classifying a possessive noun, both jobs will be recognized by labeling it as a possessive noun adjective. Use the abbreviation **PNA** (possessive noun adjective).
5. Include possessive nouns when you are asked to identify possessive nouns or adjectives. Do not include possessive nouns when you are asked to identify regular nouns.
6. To find a possessive noun, begin with the question *whose*. (*Whose car? Kim's - PNA*)

Reference 22: Sample Paragraphs in Time-Order Form

Topic: My favorite water sports **3-points:** 1. water skiing 2. swimming 3. canoeing

Example 1: Three-point paragraph using a standard topic sentence with time-order points

    I am interested in three different water sports. These water sports are water skiing, swimming, and canoeing. **<u>First</u>,** I am interested in water skiing. I like the excitement of water skiing behind a fast boat. **<u>Second</u>,** I am interested in swimming. I enjoy trying a variety of different swimming strokes. **<u>Third</u>,** I am interested in canoeing. (or **<u>Finally</u>,** *I am interested in canoeing.*) I especially like canoeing over the rapids because it is exhilarating. My three favorite water sports provide a lot of fun for me, and they keep me physically fit.

Example 2: Three-point paragraph using a standard topic sentence with time-order points

    I am interested in three different water sports. These water sports are water skiing, swimming, and canoeing. **<u>First</u>,** I am interested in water skiing. I like the excitement of water skiing behind a fast boat. **<u>Next</u>,** I am interested in swimming. I enjoy trying a variety of different swimming strokes. **<u>Last</u>,** I am interested in canoeing. (or **<u>Finally</u>,** *I am interested in canoeing.*) I especially like canoeing over the rapids because it is exhilarating. My three favorite water sports provide a lot of fun for me, and they keep me physically fit.

Reference 22: Sample Paragraphs in Time-Order Form, Continued

<u>Example 3:</u> Three-point paragraph using a general topic sentence with standard points

I enjoy participating in several water sports. Three of these sports are water skiing, swimming, and canoeing. <u>My first</u> favorite water sport is water skiing. I like the excitement of water skiing behind a fast boat. <u>My second</u> favorite water sport is swimming. I enjoy trying a variety of different swimming strokes. <u>My third</u> favorite water sport is canoeing. I especially like canoeing over the rapids because it is exhilarating. My three favorite water sports provide a lot of fun for me, and they keep me physically fit.

<u>Example 4:</u> Three-point paragraph using a general topic sentence with time-order points

I enjoy participating in water sports of all kinds. Three of these sports are water skiing, swimming, and canoeing. <u>First,</u> I am interested in water skiing. I like the excitement of water skiing behind a fast boat. <u>Next,</u> I am interested in swimming. I enjoy trying a variety of different swimming strokes. <u>Last,</u> I am interested in canoeing. (or **Finally**, *I am interested in canoeing.*) I especially like canoeing over the rapids because it is exhilarating. My three favorite water sports provide a lot of fun for me, and they keep me physically fit.

Reference 23: Irregular Verb Chart

PRESENT	PAST	PAST PARTICIPLE		PRESENT PARTICIPLE	
become	became	(has)	become	(is)	becoming
blow	blew	(has)	blown	(is)	blowing
break	broke	(has)	broken	(is)	breaking
bring	brought	(has)	brought	(is)	bringing
burst	burst	(has)	burst	(is)	bursting
buy	bought	(has)	bought	(is)	buying
choose	chose	(has)	chosen	(is)	choosing
come	came	(has)	come	(is)	coming
drink	drank	(has)	drunk	(is)	drinking
drive	drove	(has)	driven	(is)	driving
eat	ate	(has)	eaten	(is)	eating
fall	fell	(has)	fallen	(is)	falling
fly	flew	(has)	flown	(is)	flying
freeze	froze	(has)	frozen	(is)	freezing
get	got	(has)	gotten	(is)	getting
give	gave	(has)	given	(is)	giving
grow	grew	(has)	grown	(is)	growing
know	knew	(has)	known	(is)	knowing
lie	lay	(has)	lain	(is)	lying
lay	laid	(has)	laid	(is)	laying
make	made	(has)	made	(is)	making
ride	rode	(has)	ridden	(is)	riding
ring	rang	(has)	rung	(is)	ringing
rise	rose	(has)	risen	(is)	rising
sell	sold	(has)	sold	(is)	selling
sing	sang	(has)	sung	(is)	singing
sink	sank	(has)	sunk	(is)	sinking
set	set	(has)	set	(is)	setting
sit	sat	(has)	sat	(is)	sitting
shoot	shot	(has)	shot	(is)	shooting
swim	swam	(has)	swum	(is)	swimming
take	took	(has)	taken	(is)	taking
tell	told	(has)	told	(is)	telling
throw	threw	(has)	thrown	(is)	throwing
wear	wore	(has)	worn	(is)	wearing
write	wrote	(has)	written	(is)	writing

Reference 24: Homonym Chart

Homonyms are words which sound the same but have different meanings and different spellings.

1. **capital** - upper part, main	15. **lead** - metal	29. **their** - belonging to them
2. **capitol** - statehouse	16. **led** - guided	30. **there** - in that place
3. **coarse** - rough	17. **no** - not so	31. **they're** - they are
4. **course** - route/a class	18. **know** - to understand	32. **threw** - did throw
5. **council** - assembly	19. **right** - correct	33. **through** - from end to end
6. **counsel** - advice	20. **write** - to form letters	34. **to** - toward, a preposition
7. **forth** - forward	21. **principle** - a truth/rule/law	35. **too** - denoting excess
8. **fourth** - ordinal number	22. **principal** - chief/head person	36. **two** - a couple
9. **its** - possessive pronoun	23. **stationary** - motionless	37. **your** - belonging to you
10. **it's** - it is	24. **stationery** - paper	38. **you're** - you are
11. **hear** - to listen	25. **peace** - quiet	39. **weak** - not strong
12. **here** - in this place	26. **piece** - a part	40. **week** - seven days
13. **knew** - understood	27. **sent** - caused to go	41. **days** - more than one day
14. **new** - not old	28. **scent** - odor	42. **daze** - a confused state

Examples: Underline the correct homonym.

1. Matthew is a member of the student (**council**, counsel) at his school.
2. Mr. Jones (councils, **counsels**) the employees about their job opportunities.

Reference 25: Three-Point Paragraph and Essay

Outline of a Three-Point Paragraph

I. Title
II. Paragraph   (9 sentences)
   A. Topic sentence
   B. A three-point sentence
   C. A **first-point** sentence
   D. A **supporting** sentence for the first point
   E. A **second-point** sentence
   F. A **supporting** sentence for the second point
   G. A **third-point** sentence
   H. A **supporting** sentence for the third point
   I. A concluding sentence

Outline of a Three-Paragraph Essay

I. Title
II. Paragraph 1 - Introduction   *(3 sentences)*
   A. Topic and general number sentence
   B. Extra information about the topic sentence
   C. Enumeration sentence
III. Paragraph 2 - Body   *(6-9 sentences)*
   A. **First-point** sentence
   B. One or two **supporting** sentences for the first point
   C. **Second-point** sentence
   D. One or two **supporting** sentences for the second point
   E. **Third-point** sentence
   F. One or two **supporting** sentences for the third point
IV. Paragraph 3 - Conclusion   *(2 sentences)*
   A. Concluding general statement
   B. Concluding summary sentence

Reference 26: Steps in Writing a Three-Paragraph Expository Essay

WRITING TOPIC: Winter Activities That I Enjoy

ENUMERATE THE TOPIC

◆ Select three points to enumerate about the topic. **(1. sledding   2. ice skating   3. skiing)**

WRITING THE INTRODUCTION AND TITLE

1. Sentence #1 - Topic Sentence
    Write the topic sentence by using the words in your topic and adding a general number word, such as *several, many, some,* or *numerous,* instead of the exact number of points you will discuss.
    (When the weather gets cold, there are several winter activities that I enjoy.)

2. Sentence #2 - Extra Information about the topic sentence
    This sentence can clarify, explain, define, or just be an extra interesting comment about the topic sentence. If you need another sentence to complete your information, write an extra sentence here. If you write an extra sentence, your introductory paragraph will have four sentences in it instead of three sentences. **(Although some of these activities are not available in my community, I am still able to do the ones I enjoy the most.)**

3. Sentence #3 - Enumeration sentence
    This sentence will list the three points to be discussed in the order that you will present them in the Body of your paper. You can list the points with or without the specific number in front.
    (My three favorites are sledding, ice skating, and skiing.) or **(I love to go sledding, ice skating, and skiing.)**

◆ The Title - Since there are many possibilities for titles, look at the topic and the three points listed about the topic. Use some of the words in the topic and write a phrase to tell what your paragraph is about. Your title can be short or long. Capitalize the first, last, and important words in your title. **(Winter Fun)**

WRITING THE BODY

4. Sentence #4 - First Point - Write a sentence stating your first point.
    (The first winter activity that I enjoy is sledding.)

5. Sentence #5 - Supporting Sentence(s) - Write one or two sentences that give more information about your first point.
    (All the kids in our town go sledding down a long hill near my house.)

6. Sentence #6 - Second Point - Write a sentence stating your second point.
    (The second winter activity that I enjoy is ice skating.)

7. Sentence #7 - Supporting Sentence(s) - Write one or two sentences that give more information about your second point. **(Each winter, my cousins and I can hardly wait for my uncle's pond to freeze over so we can go ice skating.)**

8. Sentence #8 - Third Point - Write a sentence stating your third point.
    (The third winter activity that I enjoy is skiing.)

9. Sentence #9 - Supporting Sentence(s) - Write one or two sentences that give more information about your third point.
    (Every winter, I go to the mountains in Colorado on a ski trip with a youth group.)

Reference 26: Steps in Writing a Three-Paragraph Expository Essay, Continued

WRITING THE CONCLUSION

10. <u>Sentence #10 - Concluding General Statement</u> - Read the topic sentence again and then rewrite it using some of the same words to say the same thing in a different way.
(There are many winter activities that provide fun during cold weather.)

11. <u>Sentence #11 - Concluding Summary (Final) Sentence</u> - Read the enumeration sentence again and then rewrite it using some of the same words to say the same thing in a different way.
(I do not always get involved in as many winter activities as I would like, but the three that I enjoy most are sledding, ice skating, and skiing.)

SAMPLE THREE-PARAGRAPH ESSAY

Winter Fun

When the weather gets cold, there are several winter activities that I enjoy. Although some of these activities are not available in my community, I am still able to do the ones I enjoy the most. My three favorites are sledding, ice skating, and skiing.

The first winter activity that I enjoy is sledding. All the kids in our town go sledding down a long hill near my house. The second winter activity that I enjoy is ice skating. Each winter, my cousins and I can hardly wait for my uncle's pond to freeze over so we can go ice skating. The third winter activity that I enjoy is skiing. Every winter, I go to the mountains in Colorado on a ski trip with a youth group.

There are many winter activities that provide fun during cold weather. I do not always get involved in as many winter activities as I would like, but the three that I enjoy most are sledding, ice skating, and skiing.

Reference 27: This reference is located on page 22.

Reference 28: Sentence Parts That Can Be Used for a Pattern 1 Sentence

1. **Nouns**
   Use <u>only</u> subject nouns or object of the preposition nouns.

2. **Adverbs**
   Tell how, when, or where.
   Can be placed before or after verbs, at the beginning or end of a sentence, and in front of adjectives or other adverbs.

3. **Adjectives**
   Tell what kind, which one, or how many.
   Can be placed in front of nouns. Sometimes two or three adjectives can modify the same noun.
   Articles
   Adjectives that are used in front of nouns (a, an, the).

4. **Verbs** (Can include helping verbs.)

5. **Prepositional Phrases**
   Can be placed before or after nouns, after verbs, adverbs, or other prepositional phrases, and at the beginning or end of a sentence.

6. **Pronouns**
   (subjective, possessive, or objective)

7. **Conjunctions**
   Connecting words for compound parts: and, or, but.

8. **Interjections**
   Usually found at the beginning of a sentence. Can show strong or mild emotion.

Reference 27: Capitalization Rules

SECTION 1: CAPITALIZE THE FIRST WORD

1. The first word of a sentence. (*He likes to take a nap.*)
2. The first word in the greeting and closing of letters. (*Dear, Yours truly*)
3. The first and last word and important words in titles of literary works.
   (*books, songs, short stories, poems, articles, movie titles, magazines*)
   (*Note: Conjunctions, articles, and prepositions with fewer than five letters are not capitalized unless they are the first or last word.*)
4. The first word of a direct quotation. (*Dad said, "We are going home."*)
5. The first word in each line of a topic outline.

SECTION 2: CAPITALIZE NAMES, INITIALS, AND TITLES OF PEOPLE

6. The pronoun I. (*May I go with you?*)
7. The names and nicknames of people. (*Sam, Joe, Jones, Slim, Shorty*)
8. Family names when used in place of or with the person's name.
   (*Grandmother, Auntie, Uncle Joe, Mother – Do NOT capitalize my mother.*)
9. Titles used with, or in place of, people's names.
   (*Mr., Ms., Miss, Dr. Smith, Doctor, Captain, President, Sir*)
10. People's initials. (*J.D., C. Smith*)

SECTION 3: CAPITALIZE WORDS OF TIME

11. The days of the week and months of the year. (*Monday, July*)
12. The names of holidays. (*Christmas, Thanksgiving, Easter*)
13. The names of historical events, periods, laws, documents, conflicts, and distinguished awards.
    (*Civil War, Middle Ages, Medal of Honor*)

SECTION 4: CAPITALIZE NAMES OF PLACES

14. The names and abbreviations of cities, towns, counties, states, countries, and nations.
    (*Dallas, Texas, Fulton County, Africa, America, USA, AR, TX*)
15. The names of avenues, streets, roads, highways, routes, and post office boxes.
    (*Main Street, Jones Road, Highway 89, Rt. 1, Box 2, P.O. Box 45*)
16. The names of lakes, rivers, oceans, mountain ranges, deserts, parks, stars, planets, and constellations.
    (*Beaver Lake, Rocky Mountains, Venus*)
17. The names of schools and specific school courses.
    (*Walker Elementary School, Mathematics II*)
18. North, south, east, and west when they refer to sections of the country.
    (*up North, live in the East, out West*)

SECTION 5: CAPITALIZE NAMES OF OTHER NOUNS AND PROPER ADJECTIVES

19. The names of pets. (*Spot, Tweety Bird, etc.*)
20. The names of products. (*Campbell's soup, Kelly's chili, Ford cars, etc.*)
21. The names of companies, buildings, stores, ships, planes, space ships.
    (*Empire State Building, Titanic, IBM, The Big Tire Co.*)
22. Proper adjectives. (*the English language, Italian restaurant, French test*)
23. The names of clubs, organizations, or groups. (*Lion's Club, Jaycees, Beatles*)
24. The names of political parties, religious preferences, nationalities, and races.
    (*Democratic party, Republican, Jewish synagogue, American*)

Reference 29A: Punctuation Rules

SECTION 1: END MARK PUNCTUATION

1. Use a (.) for the end punctuation of a sentence that makes a statement.
   (*Mom baked us a cake.*)
2. Use a (?) for the end punctuation of a sentence that asks a question.
   (*Are you going to town*?)
3. Use an (!) for the end punctuation of a sentence that expresses strong feeling.
   (*That bee stung me*!)
4. Use a (.) for the end punctuation of a sentence that gives a command or makes a request.
   (*Close the door.*)

SECTION 2: COMMAS TO SEPARATE TIME WORDS

5. Use a comma between the day of the week and the month. (*Friday, July 23*)
   Use a comma between the day and year. (*July 23, 2009*)
6. Use a comma to separate the year from the rest of the sentence when the year follows the month or the month and the day.
   (*We spent May, 2001, with Mom. We spent July 23, 2001, with Dad.*)

SECTION 3: COMMAS TO SEPARATE PLACE WORDS

7. Use a comma to separate the city from the state or country.
   (*I will go to Dallas, Texas. He is from Paris, France.*)
8. Use a comma to separate the state or country from the rest of the sentence when the name of the state or country follows the name of a city.
   (*We flew to Dallas, Texas, in June. We flew to Paris, France, in July.*)

SECTION 4: COMMAS TO MAKE MEANINGS CLEAR

9. Use a comma to separate words or phrases in a series.
   (*We had soup, crackers, and milk.*)
10. Use commas to separate introductory words such as *Yes, Well, Oh,* and *No* from the rest of a sentence.
    (*Oh, I didn't know that.*)
11. Use commas to set off most appositives. An appositive is a word, phrase, title, or degree used directly after another word to explain or rename it.
    (*Sue, the girl next door, likes to draw.*)
    One-word appositives can be written two different ways: *(1) My brother, Tim, is riding in the horse show. (2) My brother Tim is riding in the horse show.* Your assignments will require one-word appositives to be set off with commas.
12. Use commas to separate a noun of direct address (the name of a person directly spoken to) from the rest of the sentence.
    (*Mom, do I really have to go?*)

SECTION 5: PUNCTUATION IN GREETINGS AND CLOSINGS OF LETTERS

13. Use a comma (,) after the salutation (greeting) of a friendly letter. (*Dear Sam,*)
14. Use a comma (,) after the closing of any letter. (*Yours truly,*)
15. Use a colon (:) after the salutation (greeting) of a business letter. (*Dear Madam:*)

Reference 29B: Punctuation Rules

SECTION 6: PERIODS

16. Use a period after most abbreviations or titles that are accepted in formal writing. (*Mr., Ms., Dr., Capt., St., Ave., St. Louis*) (*Note: These abbreviations cannot be used by themselves. They must always be used with a proper noun.*)

    In the abbreviations of many well-known organizations or words, periods are not required. (*USA, GM, TWA, GTE, AT&T, TV, AM, FM, GI, etc.*) Use only one period after an abbreviation at the end of a statement. Do not put an extra period for the end mark punctuation.

17. Use a period after initials. (*C. Smith, D.J. Brewton, Thomas A. Jones*)

18. Place a period after Roman numerals, Arabic numbers, and letters of the alphabet in an outline. (*II., IV., 5., 25., A., B.*)

SECTION 7: APOSTROPHES

19. Form a contraction by using an apostrophe in place of a letter or letters that have been left out. (*I'll, he's, isn't, wasn't, can't*)

20. Form the possessive of singular and plural nouns by using an apostrophe. (*boy's basketball, boys' basketball, children's basketball*)

21. Form the plurals of letters, symbols, numbers, and signs with the apostrophe plus *s* (*'s*). (*9's, B's, b's*)

SECTION 8: UNDERLINING

22. Use underlining or italics for titles of books, magazines, works of art, ships, newspapers, motion pictures, etc. (*A famous movie is* <u>Gone With the Wind</u>. *Our newspaper is the* <u>Cabot Star Herald</u>.) (<u>Titanic</u>, <u>Charlotte's Web</u>, etc.)

SECTION 9: QUOTATION MARKS

23. Use quotation marks to set off the titles of songs, short stories, short poems, articles, essays, short plays, and book chapters. (*Do you like to sing the song "America" in music class*?)

24. Quotation marks are used at the beginning and end of the person's words to separate what the person actually said from the rest of the sentence. Since the quotation tells what is being said, it will always have quotation marks around it.

25. The words that tell who is speaking are the explanatory words. Do not set explanatory words off with quotation marks. (*Fred said, "I'm here."*) (**Fred said** *is explanatory and should not be set off with quotations.*)

26. A new paragraph is used to indicate a change of speaker.

27. When a speaker's speech is longer than one paragraph, quotation marks are used at the beginning of each paragraph and at the end of the last paragraph of that speaker's speech.

28. Use single quotation marks to enclose a quotation within a quotation. *"My teddy bear says 'I love you' four different ways," said little Amy.*

29. Use a period at the end of explanatory words that come at the end of a sentence.

30. Use a comma to separate a direct quotation from the explanatory words.

Reference 30: Capitalization and Punctuation Examples

```
     1    6      14      14        11
1. Yes, I'll go to Lincoln, Nebraska, in July for our family reunion.
   10 19         7        8                        1
```

Editing Guide for Sample 1 Sentence: Capitals: 5   Commas: 3   Apostrophes: 1   End Marks: 1

```
     N   P
2. no, peaches, our neighbor's new golden retriever, is not a house dog.
```

Editing Guide for Sample 2 Sentence: Capitals: 2   Commas: 3   Apostrophes: 1   End Marks: 1

Reference 31: Three- Paragraph Essay and Five-Paragraph Essay

Outline of a 3-Paragraph Essay	Outline of a 5-Paragraph Essay
I. Title	I. Title

II. Paragraph 1 – Introduction (3 sentences)
  A. Topic and general number sentence
  B. Extra information about the topic sentence
  C. Enumeration sentence
	II. Paragraph 1 – Introduction (3 sentences)
	  A. Topic and general number sentence
	  B. Extra information about the topic sentence
	  C. Enumeration sentence

III. Paragraph 2 – Body   (6-9 sentences)
  A. **First-point** sentence
  B. One or two **supporting** sentences
     for the first point
  C. **Second-point** sentence
  D. One or two **supporting** sentence
     for the second point
  E. **Third-point** sentence
  F. One or two **supporting** sentences
     for the third point
	III. Paragraph 2 – First Point *(Body)* (3-4 sentences)
	  A. **First-point** sentence
	  B. Two or three **supporting** sentences for the first point
	
	IV. Paragraph 3 – Second Point *(Body)*(3-4 sentences)
	  A. **Second-point** sentence
	  B. Two or three **supporting** sentences for the second
	     point
	
	V. Paragraph 4 – Third Point *(Body)* (3-4 sentences)
	  A. **Third-point** sentence
	  B. Two or three **supporting** sentences for the third point

IV. Paragraph 3 – Conclusion   (2 sentences)
  A. Concluding general statement
  B. Concluding summary sentence
	VI. Paragraph 5 – Conclusion (2 sentences)
	  A. Concluding general statement
	     (Restatement of the topic sentence)
	  B. Concluding summary sentence
	     (Restatement of the enumeration sentence)

Reference 32: Steps in Writing a Five-Paragraph Expository Essay

WRITING TOPIC: Winter Activities That I Enjoy

ENUMERATE THE TOPIC

♦ Select the points to enumerate about the topic. **(1. sledding 2. ice skating 3. skiing)**

WRITING THE INTRODUCTION AND TITLE

1. Sentence #1 - Topic Sentence
   Write the topic sentence by using the words in your topic and adding a general number word, such as *several, many, some,* or *numerous,* instead of the exact number of points you will discuss.
   (When the weather gets cold, there are several winter activities that I enjoy.)

2. Sentence #2 - Extra Information about the topic sentence
   This sentence can clarify, explain, define, or just be an extra interesting comment about the topic sentence. If you need another sentence to complete your information, write an extra sentence here. If you write an extra sentence, your introductory paragraph will have four sentences instead of three and that is okay. **(Although some of these activities are not available in my community, I am still able to do the ones I enjoy the most.)**

3. Sentence #3 - Enumeration sentence
   This sentence will list the three points to be discussed in the order that you will present them in the body of your paper. You can list the points with or without the specific number in front.
   (My three favorite activities are sledding, ice skating, and skiing.) or **(I love to go sledding, ice skating, and skiing.)**

   ♦ The Title - Since there are many possibilities for titles, look at the topic and the three points listed about the topic. Use some of the words in the topic and write a phrase to tell what your paragraph is about. Your title can be short or long. Capitalize the first, last, and important words in your title. **(Winter Fun Begins with the Letter S)**

WRITING THE BODY

4. Sentence #4 - First Point - Write a sentence stating your first point.
   (The first winter activity that I enjoy is sledding.)

5. Sentences #5 - #7 - Supporting Sentences - Write two or three sentences that give more information about your first point. **(There is a long hill behind my house that glazes over every time it snows.) (People from all over town gather there, and we all go sledding.) (It's great to feel the rush of excitement as several sleds push off to race to the bottom.)**

6. Sentence #8 - Second Point - Write a sentence stating your second point.
   (The second winter activity that I enjoy is ice skating.)

7. Sentences #9 - #11 - Supporting Sentences - Write two or three sentences that give more information about your second point. **(If the weather gets cold enough, my uncle's pond freezes over and is thick enough to support skaters.) (My cousins and I love to skate on that pond.) (We are not professionals, but we have lots of fun making figure 8's and doing our version of the triple axle.)**

Reference 32: Steps in Writing a Five-Paragraph Expository Essay (continued)

8. <u>Sentence #12 - Third Point</u> - Write a sentence stating your third point.
   (The third winter activity that I enjoy is skiing.)

9. <u>Sentences #13 - #15 - Supporting Sentences</u> - Write two or three sentences that give more information about your third point. **(Although there are no mountains nearby on which I can ski, there is almost always a ski trip with a youth group.) (On a ski trip, I get a chance to try out all kinds of slopes from "easy" to "dangerous.") (If I don't "wipe out" on a tree, I have a wonderful time skiing.)**

WRITING THE CONCLUSION

10. <u>Sentence #16 - Concluding General Statement</u> - Read the topic sentence again and then rewrite it using some of the same words to say the same thing in a different way. **(There are many winter activities that provide fun during cold weather.)**

11. <u>Sentence #17 - Concluding Summary Sentence</u> - Read the enumeration sentence again and then rewrite it, using some of the same words to say the same thing in a different way. **(I do not always get involved in as many winter activities as I would like, but the three that I enjoy most are sledding, ice skating, and skiing.)**

SAMPLE FIVE-PARAGRAPH ESSAY

Winter Fun Begins with the Letter <u>S</u>

When the weather gets cold, there are several winter activities that I enjoy. Although some of these activities are not available in my community, I am still able to do the ones I enjoy the most. My three favorite activities are sledding, ice skating, and skiing.

The first winter activity that I enjoy is sledding. There is a long hill behind my house that glazes over every time it snows. People from all over town gather there, and we all go sledding. It's great to feel the rush of excitement as several sleds push off to race to the bottom.

The second winter activity that I enjoy is ice skating. If the weather gets cold enough, my uncle's pond freezes over and is thick enough to support skaters. My cousins and I love to skate on that pond. We are not professionals, but we have lots of fun making figure 8's and doing our version of the triple axle.

The third winter activity that I enjoy is skiing. Although there are no mountains nearby on which I can ski, there is almost always a ski trip with a youth group. On a ski trip, I get a chance to try out all kinds of slopes from "easy" to "dangerous." If I don't "wipe out" on a tree, I have a wonderful time skiing.

There are many winter activities that provide fun during cold weather. I do not always get involved in as many winter activities as I would like, but the three that I enjoy most are sledding, ice skating, and skiing.

Reference 33: Persuasive Paragraph and Essay Guidelines

Guidelines for a Persuasive Paragraph	Guidelines for a 3-Paragraph Persuasive Essay

Paragraph (10-13 sentences)
A. **Topic** sentence (opinion statement)
B. **General number** sentence
C. **First-point** persuasive sentence
D. 1 or 2 **supporting** sentences for the first point
E. **Second-point** persuasive sentence
F. 1 or 2 **supporting** sentences for the second point
G. **Third-point** persuasive sentence
H. 1 or 2 **supporting** sentences for the third point
I. **In conclusion** sentence (Repeat topic idea)
J. **Final summary** sentence (Summarize reasons)
	1. Paragraph 1 – Introduction (3 sentences)
	  A. **Topic** sentence (opinion statement)
	  B. **Reason** sentence
	  C. **General number** sentence
	2. Paragraph 2 – Body (6-9 sentences)
	  A. **First-point** persuasive sentence
	  B. 1 or 2 **supporting** sentences for the first point
	  C. **Second-point** persuasive sentence
	  D. 1 or 2 **supporting** sentences for the second point
	  E. **Third-point** persuasive sentence
	  F. 1 or 2 **supporting** sentences for the third point
	3. Paragraph 3 - Conclusion (2 sentences)
	  A. **In conclusion** sentence (Repeat topic idea)
	  B. **Final summary** sentence (Summarize reasons)

Radar Tracking System

Every local radio station should have a radar tracking system. This system could be used to keep its listeners informed about local weather conditions. There are numerous benefits from local weather radar systems.

The first benefit from local weather radar is for advance warning about high-intensity thunderstorms with possible hail. Such a warning can alert listeners to disconnect costly appliances and secure cars and other vehicles under cover. The second benefit from local weather radar is for tornado sightings. Those who are given warning of a twister on the ground can take shelter and even save their lives. The third benefit from local weather radar is a simple sense of security. A community that has a weather-warning defense system feels more secure.

In conclusion, local radio stations need weather-radar tracking systems. By providing their listeners with such systems, they increase their patrons' security.

Reference 34: Direct Object, Verb-transitive, and Pattern 2

1. A **direct object** is a noun or pronoun after the verb that completes the meaning of the sentence.

2. A **direct object** is labeled as **DO**.

3. To find the **direct object**, ask WHAT or WHOM after the verb.

4. A **direct object** must be verified to mean someone or something different from the subject noun.

5. A **verb-transitive** is an action verb with a direct object after it and is labeled V-t. (Whatever receives the action of a transitive verb is the direct object.)

Sample Sentence for the exact words to say to find the direct object and transitive verb.

1. Dave builds a snowman.
2. Who builds a snowman? Dave - SN
3. What is being said about Dave? Dave builds - V
4. Dave builds what? snowman - verify the noun
5. Does snowman mean the same thing as Dave? No.
6. Snowman - DO *(Say: Snowman - direct object.)*
7. Builds - V-t *(Say: Builds - verb-transitive.)*
8. A - A

9. SN V-t DO P2 Check *(Say: Subject Noun, Verb-transitive, Direct Object, Pattern 2, Check.) (This first check is to make sure the "t" is added to the verb.)*
10. Verb-transitive - check again. *("Check again" means to check for prepositional phrases and then go through the rest of the Question and Answer Flow.)*
11. No prepositional phrases.
12. Period, statement, declarative sentence
13. Go back to the verb - divide the complete subject from the complete predicate.
14. Is there an adverb exception? No.
15. Is this sentence in a natural or inverted order? Natural - no change.

Reference 35: Regular Editing Checklist

Read each sentence and go through the Sentence Checkpoints below.

_____ E1. Sentence sense check. (Check for words left out or words repeated.)

_____ E2. First word, capital letter check. End mark check. Any other capitalization check. Any other punctuation check.

_____ E3. Sentence structure and punctuation check. (Check for correct construction and correct punctuation of a simple sentence, a simple sentence with compound parts, a compound sentence, or a complex sentence.)

_____ E4. Spelling and homonym check. (Check for misspelled words and incorrect homonym choices.)

_____ E5. Usage check. (Check subject-verb agreement, a/an choice, pronoun/antecedent agreement, pronoun cases, degrees of adjectives, double negatives, verb tenses, and contractions.)

Read each paragraph and go through the Paragraph Checkpoints below.

_____ E6. Check to see that each paragraph is indented.

_____ E7. Check each paragraph for a topic sentence.

_____ E8. Check each sentence to make sure it supports the topic of the paragraph.

_____ E9. Check the content for interest and creativity. Do not begin all sentences with the same word, and use a variety of simple, compound, and complex sentences.

_____ E10. Check the type and format of the writing assigned.

Reference 36: This reference is located on page 30.

Reference 37: Complete Sentences and Sentence Fragments

Part 1

Identifying simple sentences and fragments: Write **S** for a complete sentence and **F** for a sentence fragment on the line beside each group of words below.

S	1.	The children sang sweetly.
F	2.	In the world.
S	3.	Ducks quacked.
F	4.	Running toward the goal.
F	5.	The huge rocks.

Part 2

Fragment Examples: (1) singing in the shower (2) two red birds in the tree (3) as I walked in the park (4) for a ticket to the game.

Reference 37: Complete Sentences and Sentence Fragments (continued)

Part 3
Directions: Add the part that is underlined in parentheses to make each fragment into a complete sentence.

1. At the edge of the pond for a drink of water. (subject part, predicate part, <u>both the subject and predicate</u>)
   (The thirsty lion stood fearlessly at the edge of the pond for a drink of water.)

2. A pack of hungry wolves. (subject part, <u>predicate part</u>, both the subject and predicate)
   (A pack of hungry wolves **growled ferociously at the group of rabbits**.)

3. Was yelling and running toward the burning house. (<u>subject part</u>, predicate part, both the subject and predicate)
   (The frantic father was yelling and running toward the burning house.)

Reference 36: Editing Example

Topic: **Reasons cowboys use quarter horses** Three main points: **(1. speed 2. quickness 3. endurance)**

Cowboys
Quarter Horses for cowboy

→(indent)　　　　A　　　　　　　　　　　　　　　　　(.) A
Cowboys of the american West like quarter horses for several reasons although quarter horses are widely
　　　　different　　　　　　　　　　　　　　　　　　　　　**reasons**
used for diferent purposes, it is the cowboy who has made quarter horses so famous. Three reason
　　　　　　　their　　**their**　　　　　**their**　　　(.)
cowboys use quarter horses are its speed, its quickness, and its endurance
　　　　　　　　　　　　　　　their speed　　　　　　**their**
　　The first reason that cowboys use quarter horses is there. Quarter horses got its name
　　they're
because their able to run at great speeds for short distances. The second reason that cowboys use
　　　　their　　　　　　**have**
quarter horses is there quickness. They the ability to stop and start quickly. A quarter
horse's　　　　　　　　　　　　　　　　**calves**
horses quickness makes it easy for cowboys to separate cows or calfs from the rest of the cattle or to
　　　　　herd　　　　　　　　　　　　　　　**their**
guide strays back to the heard. The third reason that cowboys use quarter horses is there endurance.
　　　are　　　　　　　　　　　　　　　　　　(.)
Quarter horses is able to work for long periods of time with little or no rest
　　　　　　　　　　　　　　　reasons　　　　　　(,)
　　In conclusion, cowboys use quarter horses for many reason. The quarter horses' speed quickness, and
endurance make　　　　　　　　　　A　　　　(.)
endurance makes them valuable horses to the american cowboy

Total Mistakes: 30
Editing Guide: Sentence checkpoints: E1, E2, E3, E4, E5　　Paragraph checkpoints: E6, E7, E8, E9, E10

Reference 38: Simple Sentences, Compound Parts, and Fragments

Part 1:
Example 1: The puppy looked shyly at his owner. **(S)**　　**Example 2:** Sam's <u>mom and dad</u> drove to Texas. **(SCS)**

Example 3: Laura <u>sang and danced</u> in the play. **(SCV)**

Part 2: Identify each kind of sentence by writing the abbreviation in the blank. **(S, SS, F, SCS, SCV)**

<u>SCV</u> 1. They jogged and walked down the trail.　　　<u>S</u> 4. I mowed the yard yesterday.
<u>SCS</u> 2. The boys and girls ran outside.　　　　　　<u>SS</u> 5. Jimmy went to the party. He had a good time.
<u>F</u> 3. After the storm last night.

Part 3: Put a slash to separate each run-on sentence below. Then, correct the run-on sentences by rewriting them as indicated by the labels in parentheses at the end of each sentence.

1. The baby birds were chirping / they were hungry. **(SS)**
   The baby birds were chirping. They were hungry.
2. The milk is in the refrigerator / the butter is in the refrigerator. **(SCS)**
   The milk and butter are in the refrigerator.
3. The lifeguard jumped up / he dove into the pool. **(SCV)**
   The lifeguard jumped up and dove into the pool.

Reference 39: The Compound Sentence

1. Compound means two. A compound sentence is two complete sentences joined together correctly.

2. <u>The first way to join two sentences</u> to make a compound sentence is to <u>use a comma and a conjunction</u>. The formula for you to follow will always be given at the end of the sentence. The formula gives the abbreviation for compound sentence and lists the conjunction to use (**CD, but**). Remember to place the comma BEFORE the conjunction.

   Example: I looked for my **keys, but** I could not find them. (**CD**, but)

3. <u>The second way to join two sentences</u> and make a compound sentence is to <u>use a semicolon and a connective (conjunctive) adverb</u>. The formula to follow is given at the end of the sentence. The formula gives the abbreviation for compound sentence and lists the connective adverb to use (**CD; however,**). Remember to place a semicolon BEFORE the connective adverb and a comma AFTER the connective adverb.

   Example: I looked for my keys**; however,** I could not find them. (**CD**; however,)

4. <u>The third way to join two sentences</u> and make a compound sentence is to <u>use a semicolon only</u>. The formula to follow is given at the end of the sentence and lists the semicolon after the abbreviation for compound sentence (**CD;**). Remember, there is no conjunction or connective adverb when the semicolon is used alone.

   Example: I looked for my **keys;** I could not find them. (**CD;**)

5. Compound sentences should be closely related in thought and importance.
   <u>Correct:</u>   I looked for my **keys, but** I could not find them.
   <u>Incorrect:</u> I looked for my keys, but I failed my science test today.

Reference 40: Coordinate Conjunction and Connective Adverb Chart

Type of Conj / Adv	More Information	Contrast/Choice	Alternative	As a result
Coordinate Conjunction	,and ,nor	,but ,yet	,or	,so (as a result) so (that) - no comma
Connective Adverbs	;moreover, ;furthermore, ;besides, ;also, ;likewise,	;however, ;nevertheless,	;otherwise,	;therefore, ;hence, ;thus, ;consequently, ;accordingly,

Reference 41: Examples Using S, SCS, SCV, and CD to Correct Run-On Sentences

Put a slash to separate the two complete thoughts in each run-on sentence. Correct the run-on sentences or fragments as indicated by the labels in parentheses at the end of each sentence.

1. Marty enjoyed the movie **/** he didn't like the popcorn. (**CD**, but)
   Marty enjoyed the movie, but he didn't like the popcorn.

2. The young man began work at 5:00 each morning **/** he went to bed early at night. (**CD**; therefore,)
   The young man began work at 5:00 each morning; therefore, he went to bed early at night.

3. I work out every day **/** the exercise makes me feel great! (**CD;**)
   I work out every day; the exercise makes me feel great!

4. Leon sold pens to the chairman of the company. Leon sold pencils to the chairman. (**S**)
   Leon sold pens and pencils to the chairman of the company.
   (Simple sentences can have other compound parts.)

5. Kerri is at band practice until 6:00 **/** Terri is at band practice until 6:00. (**SCS**)
   Kerri and Terri are at band practice until 6:00. *(When the subject is compound, the verb is plural.)*

6. For enjoyment, Elizabeth plays the flute **/** she writes poetry. (**SCV**)
   For enjoyment, Elizabeth plays the flute and writes poetry.

Reference 42: Identifying S, F, SCS, SCV, and CD

Part 1: Identify each kind of sentence by writing the abbreviation in the blank (**S, F, SCS, SCV, CD**).

CD 1. Samuel squinted at the computer screen; however, he could not see the symbols clearly.

S 2. During the school year, Joshua participates in basketball, football, and track.

CD 3. We ate cheese and crackers for a snack, but we did not eat cookies.

SCS 4. Dana and Tommy walk two miles together every day.

F 5. In the tower, the enchanted princess with long, flowing hair.

SCV 6. My mother baked bread and muffins and boiled shrimp for our supper.

Part 2: On notebook paper, use the ways listed below to correct this run-on sentence: **The river rose it did not flood.**

7. CD, but **The river rose, but it did not flood.**   8. SCV **The river rose but did not flood.**

Reference 43: The Complex Sentence and Subordinate Conjunctions

Definition: A complex sentence is made by correctly joining two sentences: an <u>independent</u> sentence and a <u>subordinate</u> sentence.

1. **Independent sentence:** The bell rang for class.
2. **Subordinate sentence:** <u>When</u> the bell rang for class.
3. **Complex sentence:** <u>When</u> the bell rang for class, <u>the students took their seats</u>.

Example 1: the bell rang for class the students took their seats. (**CX, when**) (1)
   When the bell rang for class, the students took their seats.
Example 2: the students took their seats the bell rang for class. (**CX, after**) (2)
   The students took their seats after the bell rang for class.
Example 3: **When the bell rang for class,** the students took their seats.
Example 4: The students took their seats **when the bell rang for class.**

Review

A. A sentence becomes a complex sentence when you add a subordinate conjunction to one of the two sentences that make up a complex sentence.

B. Any independent sentence can be made subordinate (dependent) by simply adding a subordinate conjunction to the beginning of that sentence.
   Subordinate sentences: (**When** the bell rang) (**If** the bell rang) (**Before** the bell rang) (**After** the bell rang)

A LIST OF THE MOST COMMON SUBORDINATE CONJUNCTIONS

A subordinate conjunction is a conjunction that always introduces a subordinate sentence. Since there are many subordinate conjunctions, only a few of the most common subordinate conjunctions are provided in the list below.

after	because	except	so that	though	when
although	before	if	than	unless	where
as, or as soon as	even though	since	that	until	while

Reference 44: Examples of Complex Sentences

Part 1: Put a slash to separate each sentence. Rewrite and correct the run-on sentences as indicated by the labels in parentheses.	**Part 2:** Identify each kind of sentence by writing the abbreviation in the blank (**S, F, SCS, SCV, CD, CX**).
1. JoAnn got sick / she went to the doctor. (**CX, when**) (1)	5. __CX__ The dogs will not come unless you call them.
2. I worked two jobs / I needed the money. (**CX, because**) (2)	6. __SCS__ After school, the boys and girls went skating.
3. You cannot pass this test / you do not study. (**CX, if**) (2)	7. __CD__ I liked math, and my brother liked science.
4. The storm hit / we took cover. (**CX, before**) (1)	8. __SCV__ My dad planted and fertilized his crops early.
Key for 1-4: 1. When JoAnn got sick, she went to the doctor. 3. You cannot pass this test if you do not study.	2. I worked two jobs because I needed the money. 4. Before the storm hit, we took cover.

Reference 45: Making Nouns Possessive

1. For a singular noun - add ('s)	2. For a plural noun that ends in **s** - add (')	3. For a plural noun that does not end in **s** - add ('s)
Rule 1: boy's	**Rule 2: boys'**	**Rule 3: men's**

Part A: Underline each noun to be made possessive and write singular or plural (**S-P**), the rule number, and the possessive form. Part B: Write each noun as singular possessive and then as plural possessive.

Part A	S-P	Rule	Possessive Form	Part B	Singular Poss	Plural Poss
1. <u>girl</u> ring	S	1	**girl's ring**	5. boss	**boss's**	**bosses'**
2. <u>writers</u> pens	P	2	**writers' pens**	6. woman	**woman's**	**women's**
3. <u>children</u> sleds	P	3	**children's sleds**	7. wife	**wife's**	**wives'**
4. <u>deer</u> hooves	S or P	1 or 3	**deer's hooves**	8. Smith	**Smith's**	**Smiths'**

Reference 46: Indirect Object and Pattern 3

1. An **indirect object** is a noun or pronoun.

2. An **indirect object** receives what the direct object names.

3. An **indirect object** is located between the verb-transitive and the direct object.

4. An **indirect object** is labeled as **IO**.

5. To find the **indirect object**, ask TO WHOM or FOR WHOM after the direct object.

Sample Sentence for the exact words to say to find the indirect object.

1. Dave builds me a snowman.
2. Who builds me a snowman? Dave - SN
3. What is being said about Dave? Dave builds - V
4. Dave builds what? snowman - verify the noun
5. Does snowman mean the same thing as Dave? No.
6. Snowman - DO
7. Builds - V-t
8. Dave builds snowman for whom? me - IO
   (*Say: Me - indirect object.*)
9. A - A
10. SN V-t IO DO P3 Check (*Say: Subject Noun, Verb-transitive, Indirect Object, Direct Object, Pattern 3, Check.*) (*This first check is to make sure the "t" is added to the verb.*)

11. Verb-transitive - check again. (*"Check again" means to check for prepositional phrases and then go through the rest of the Question and Answer Flow.*)
12. No prepositional phrases.
13. Period, statement, declarative sentence
14. Go back to the verb - divide the complete subject from the complete predicate.
15. Is there an adverb exception? No.
16. Is this sentence in a natural or inverted order? Natural - no change.

Reference 47: Subjective, Objective, and Possessive Pronoun Cases

1. The **subject** pronouns are in the **subjective case:** *I, we, he, she, it, they,* and *you.*
   Use subjective case pronouns for subjects or predicate pronouns.

2. The **object** pronouns are in the **objective case:** *me, us, him, her, it, them,* and *you.*
   Use objective case pronouns for objects: object of a preposition, direct object, or indirect object.

3. The **possessive** pronouns are in the **possessive case:** *my, our, his, her, its, their, your,* and *mine.*
   Use possessive case pronouns to show ownership.

Practice Section: For Sentences 1-4, replace each underlined pronoun by writing the correct form in the first blank and **S** or **O** for subjective or objective case in the second blank.

1. She and <u>me</u> are riding with Tim.   I   S
2. Susan will listen to Pam and <u>I</u>.   me   O

3. Do you want <u>he and I</u> to leave?   him and me   O
4. Do you prefer <u>they or I</u>.   them or me   O

Reference 48: Quotation Rules for Beginning Quotes

1. **Pattern:** "C -quote- (,!?) " <u>explanatory words</u> (.)
   (Quotation marks, capital letter, quote, end punctuation choice, quotation marks closed, explanatory words, period.)
2. Underline **end explanatory words** and use a period at the end.
3. You should see the **beginning quote** – Use quotation marks at the beginning and end of what is said. Then, put a comma, question mark, or exclamation point (no period) after the quote but in front of the quotation mark.
4. **Capitalize** the beginning of a quote and any proper nouns or the pronoun *I*.
5. **Punctuate** the rest of the sentence by checking for any apostrophes, periods, or commas that may be needed within the sentence.

Guided Practice

Sentence: the boys and i are going hunting on friday with b j moss my dad said

1. Pattern: **"C** -quote- **(,!?) "** <u>explanatory words</u> **(.)**
2. the boys and i are going hunting on friday with b j moss **<u>my dad said</u>**(.)
3. "the boys and i are going hunting on friday with b j moss**,"** <u>my dad said</u>.
4. **"T**he boys and **I** are going hunting on **F**riday with **B J M**oss," <u>my dad said</u>.
5. "The boys and I are going hunting on Friday with B. J. Moss," <u>my dad said</u>.
6. **Corrected Sentence:** "The boys and I are going hunting on Friday with B. J. Moss," my dad said.

Reference 49: Quotation Rules for End Quotes

1. **Pattern:** <u>C -explanatory words</u>(,) **"C** -quote- **(.!?) "**
   (Capital letter, explanatory words, comma, quotation marks, capital letter, quote, end punctuation choice, quotation marks closed)
2. Underline **beginning explanatory words** and use a comma after them.
3. You should see the **end quote** – Use quotation marks at the beginning and end of what is said. Then, put a period, question mark, or exclamation point (no comma) after the quote, usually in front of the quotation mark.
4. **Capitalize** the first of the explanatory words at the beginning of a sentence, the beginning of the quote, and any proper nouns or the pronoun *I*.
5. **Punctuate** the rest of the sentence by checking for any apostrophes, periods, or commas that may be needed within the sentence.

Guided Practice

Sentence: my dad said the boys and i are going hunting on friday with b j moss

1. Pattern: <u>**C** -explanatory words</u>(,) **"C** -quote- **(.!?) "**
2. **<u>my dad said</u>(,)** the boys and i are going hunting on friday with b j moss
3. <u>my dad said</u>, "the boys and i are going hunting on friday with b j moss**. "**
4. <u>My dad said</u>, "The boys and **I** are going hunting on **F**riday with **B J M**oss."
5. <u>My dad said</u>, "The boys and I are going hunting on Friday with B**.** J. Moss."
6. **Corrected Sentence:** My dad said, "The boys and I are going hunting on Friday with B. J. Moss."

Reference 50: Quotation Rules for Split Quotes

1. **Pattern:** "C -quote- **(,)** "c –explanatory words(,) "c –quote- **(.!?)** "
   (Quotation marks, capital letter, first part of quote, comma, quotation marks, explanatory words, comma, quotation marks again, second part of quote, end punctuation choice, quotation marks.)

2. Underline **middle explanatory words** and place a comma after them.

3. You should see the **first part of a split quote** – Use quotation marks at the beginning and end of the first part of what is said. Then, put a comma after the first part of the quote but in front of the quotation mark.

4. You should see the **second part of a split quote** – Use quotation marks at the beginning and end of the second part of what is said. Then, put end mark punctuation (no comma) after the quote but usually in front of the quotation mark.

5. **Capitalize** the beginning of a quote and any proper nouns or the pronoun *I*. (Do not capitalize the first word of the second part unless it is a proper noun or the pronoun *I*.)

6. **Punctuate** the rest of the sentence by checking for any apostrophes, periods, or commas that may be needed within the sentence.

Guided Practice

Sentence: the boys and i my dad said are going hunting on friday with b j moss

1. Pattern: "C -quote- **(,)** "c –explanatory words(,) "c -quote- **(.!?)** "
2. the boys and i **my dad said**(,) are going hunting on friday with b j moss
3. "the boys and i**,**" my dad said, are going hunting on friday with b j moss
4. "the boys and i," my dad said, "are going hunting on friday with b j moss**(.)**"
5. "The boys and **I**," my dad said, "are going hunting on **F**riday with **B J M**oss."
6. "The boys and I," my dad said, "are going hunting on Friday with B. J. Moss."
7. **Corrected Sentence:** "The boys and I," my dad said, "are going hunting on Friday with B. J. Moss."

Note: When you enclose two sentences in quotation marks, you still have two sentences, not a split quote. "The boys and I are going hunting on Friday," my dad said. "I think they need the experience."

Reference 51: Other Quotation Rules

1. Longer Quotes

    A. When a quotation consists of several sentences, put quotation marks only at the beginning and at the end of the whole quotation, not around each sentence in the quotation.

        Dad said, "The boys and I are going hunting on Friday. We'll probably spend four or five hours in the woods before we come home."

    B. When one person has a lengthy quote which is longer than one paragraph, quotation marks are used at the beginning of each paragraph and at the end of the last paragraph of that speaker's quote. Then, when the speaker changes, a new paragraph is started.

        " _____

     _____ (same speaker continues)

        " _____

     _____ " (same speaker ends)

        " _____ " (new speaker begins and ends)

2. A Quote Within a Quote

Single quotation marks are used to punctuate a quotation within a quotation.

    My sister said, "Did you hear Mom say, 'Dinner is ready'?"

3. Quotation Marks to Punctuate Titles

Quotation marks are used to punctuate titles of songs, poems, short stories, chapters of books, articles, TV programs, and short plays. (_Capitalize the first word, last word, and every word except for articles, short prepositions, and short conjunctions._)

    I can recite several stanzas of "Paul Revere's Ride."

4. Direct Quotations, Indirect Quotations, and Statements

    A. A direct quotation occurs when you show exactly what someone says by using quotation marks.

        Direct quotation: Roger said, "I want a big glass of tea."

    B. An indirect quotation occurs when you simply describe what someone says without using his exact words.

        Indirect quotation: Roger said he wanted a big glass of tea.

    C. A statement occurs when no speaker is mentioned and no quotation is used.

        Statement: Roger wants a big glass of tea.

Reference 52: This reference is located on page 37.

Reference 53: Regular and Irregular Verbs

Most verbs are **regular verbs**. This means that they form the past tense merely by adding **-ed**, **-d**, or **-t** to the main verb: _race, raced_. This simple procedure makes regular verbs easy to identify. Some verbs, however, do not form their past tense in this regular way. For this reason, they are called **irregular verbs**. Most irregular verbs form the past tense by having a **vowel spelling change** in the word. For example: _sing, sang, sung_ or _eat, ate, eaten_.

To decide if a verb is regular or irregular, remember these two things:

1. Look only at the main verb. If the main verb is made past tense with an **-ed**, **-d, or -t** ending, it is a regular verb. (race, raced, raced)
2. Look only at the main verb. If the main verb is made past tense with a vowel spelling change, it is an irregular verb. (sing, sang, sung)

A partial listing of the most common irregular verbs is on the irregular verb chart located in Reference 23 on page 18. Refer to this chart whenever necessary.

Example: Identify each verb as regular or irregular and put **R** or **I** in the blank. Then, write the past tense form.

dance	R	danced	shoot	I	shot	drive	I	drove
grow	I	grew	try	R	tried	build	R	built

Reference 52: Story Elements Outline

1. **Main Idea (Tell the problem or situation that needs a solution.)**
   The writer had a swimming party planned but was grounded because of a messy room.
2. **Setting (Tell when and where the story takes place, either clearly stated or implied.)**
   When – The story takes place in the summer time. Where – The story takes place at the writer's house.
3. **Character (Tell whom or what the story is about.)**
   The main characters are the writer, her mother, and her younger brother.
4. **Plot (Tell what the characters in the story do and what happens to them.)**
   The story is about a girl who pays her younger brother to clean her room so she can go to a swimming party.
5. **Ending (Use a strong ending that will bring the story to a close.)**
   The story ends with the writer getting tricked by her younger brother.

Why Can't Growing Up Be Easy?

My friends and I had been planning tonight's swimming party for weeks. But, my mom wouldn't let me do anything until my room was spic and span. I couldn't talk on the phone, see my friends, or leave the house. Mom had been after me for days, but I saw no reason to be "Mr. Clean." Anyway, there was nothing wrong with my room. I sort of liked having everything out where I could get to it easily. Mom was just unfair! All she could say was, "You're grounded until this room is cleaned up, and that means today!"

"She treats me like a baby!" I wailed. "How am I going to get ready to go to the party and clean up this dumb room?" Then, I spotted my brother standing in the doorway. "Tommy," I coaxed, "you don't mind helping me out, do you?" As Tommy started backing away, I added, "I'll pay you five dollars if it passes Mom's inspection."

As Mom walked around my room shaking her head in disbelief, I smiled smugly and handed my brother his well-earned five dollars. He grinned and took off without a backward glance. I followed Mom around as she gave my room the white-glove treatment. I had my bag slung over my shoulder, ready to leave as soon as she gave the sign. Mom was telling me how pleased she was when she opened my closet door. My mouth fell open, and my eyes bugged out as everything I owned came crashing into the middle of my room. I just stood rooted to the spot and stared at the biggest mess in the world. In total distress, I knotted my fists, threw back my head, and screamed, "Tom—my!"

Reference 54: Simple Verb Tenses

When you are writing paragraphs, you must use verbs that are in the same tense. Tense means time. The tense of a verb shows the time of the action. There are three basic tenses that show when an action takes place. They are **present tense, past tense,** and **future tense**. These tenses are known as the simple tenses. *(Use the abbreviation irr for the word irregular.)*

1. The **simple present tense** shows that something is happening now, in the present. The present tense form usually ends in **-s, -es,** or has a *plain ending*.
   (Regular present tense form: race, races) (Irregular present tense form: fall, falls)
   (**Examples:** The cars <u>race</u> toward the finish line. The snow <u>falls</u> silently.)

2. The **simple past tense** shows that something has happened sometime in the past. The regular past tense form ends in **-ed, -d, or -t**. Most irregular past tense forms should be memorized.
   (Regular past tense form: raced) (Irregular past tense form: fell)
   (**Examples:** The cars <u>raced</u> toward the finish line. The snow <u>fell</u> silently.)

3. The **future tense** shows that something will happen sometime in the future. The future tense form always has the helping verb *will* or *shall* before the main verb.
   (Regular future tense form: will race) (Irregular future tense form: will fall)
   (**Examples:** The cars <u>will race</u> toward the finish line. The snow <u>will fall</u> silently.)

Simple Present Tense	Simple Past Tense	Simple Future Tense
What to look for: **one verb** with -s, -es, or plain ending.	What to look for: **one verb** with -ed, -d, -t or irr spelling change.	What to look for: **will** or **shall** with a main verb.
1. He <u>walks</u> to the car. 2. They <u>drive</u> the car.	3. He <u>walked</u> to the car. 4. They <u>drove</u> the car.	5. He <u>will walk</u> to the car. 6. They <u>will drive</u> the car.

Reference 55: Tenses of Helping Verbs

1. If there is only a main verb in a sentence, the tense is determined by the main verb and will be either present tense or past tense.
2. If there is a helping verb with a main verb, the tense of both verbs will be determined by the helping verb, not the main verb.

Since the helping verb determines the tense, it is important to learn the tenses of the 14 helping verbs you will be using. You should memorize the list below so you will never have trouble with tenses.

Present tense helping verbs: am, is, are, has, have, do, does
Past tense helping verbs: was, were, had, did, been
Future tense helping verbs: will, shall

If you use one of the present tense helping verbs, you are considered in present tense even though the main verb has an -ed ending and even though it doesn't sound like present tense. (*I have walked - present tense.*) In later grades, you will learn that certain helping verbs help form other tenses called the perfect tenses.

Example 1: Underline each verb or verb phrase. Identify the verb tense by writing a number **1** for present tense, a number **2** for past tense, or a number **3** for future tense. Write the past tense form and **R** or **I** for Regular or Irregular.

Verb Tense		Main Verb Past Tense Form	R or I
1	1. The student <u>gives</u> his speech.	gave	I
2	2. The detective <u>had tried</u> the wrong door.	tried	R
3	3. The man <u>will wait</u> for his change.	waited	R

Example 2: List the present tense and past tense helping verbs below.

Present tense:	1. **am**	2. **is**	3. **are**	4. **has**	5. **have**	6. **do**	7. **does**
Past tense:	8. **was**	9. **were**	10. **had**	11. **did**	12. **been**		

Reference 56: Principal Parts of Verbs

Every main verb has four principal forms, or parts. All the forms of a main verb are made by using one of the four principal parts. The four principal parts of main verbs are called **present, present participle, past,** and **past participle**. The principal parts are the same for regular and irregular verbs.

1. **Present principal part** - has a present tense main verb and no helping verb.
   (He <u>walks</u> home. They <u>walk</u> home.) (He <u>grows</u> fast. They <u>grow</u> fast.)

2. **Past principal part** - has a past tense main verb and no helping verb.
   (He <u>walked</u> home.) (He <u>grew</u> fast.)

3. **Past participle principal part** - has past tense main verb and present or past tense helping verb.
   (He <u>has walked</u> home.) (He <u>has grown</u> fast.)

4. **Present participle principal part** - has a main verb ending in -*ing* and a present or past tense helping verb.
   (He <u>is walking</u> home.) (He <u>is growing</u> fast.)

Examples: Principal parts of the regular verb *walk*: walk(s), walked, has walked, is walking
Examples: Principal parts of the irregular verb *grow*: grow(s), grew, has grown, is growing

Remember, you must not confuse the past principal part of the verb with the past participle principal part. The past principal part never has a helping verb. The past participle principal part always has a helping verb.

Reference 57: Changing Tenses in Paragraphs

Guided Example 1: Change the underlined present tense verbs in Paragraph 1 to past tense verbs in Paragraph 2.

Paragraph 1: Present Tense

Bossie **kicks** over the milk pail every morning. The warm, white milk **spills** upon the ground. Mama **talks** angrily to Bossie. Bossie **rolls** her eyes at Mama. Mama **stands** up, and she **calls** for Papa. Papa **pets** Bossie. Then, he **sits** down and **milks** her without any trouble. Bossie just **grins** at Mama.

Paragraph 2: Past Tense

Bossie **kicked** over the milk pail every morning. The warm, white milk **spilled** upon the ground. Mama **talked** angrily to Bossie. Bossie **rolled** her eyes at Mama. Mama **stood** up, and she **called** for Papa. Papa **petted** Bossie. Then, he **sat** down and **milked** her without any trouble. Bossie just **grinned** at Mama.

Guided Example 2: Change the underlined mixed tense verbs in Paragraph 1 to past tense verbs in Paragraph 2.

Paragraph 3: Mixed Tenses

I **did** not **understand** my neighbor. He **has** an "okay" yard. It never **grows** very much unless it **rained** a lot. Then, he **decides** to sod his yard. The sod **looked** like squares of carpet. He **places** them carefully in his front lawn. He **waters** and **fertilized** his lawn quite often. His beautiful lawn now **had** growing problems. It **grew** too well because he **had** to mow it every week. That **is** his problem, right? Wrong! My dad **bought** sod for our "okay" yard. Right! I **had** to mow it!

Paragraph 4: Past Tense

I **did** not **understand** my neighbor. He **had** an "okay" yard. It never **grew** very much unless it **rained** a lot. Then, he **decided** to sod his yard. The sod **looked** like squares of carpet. He **placed** them carefully in his front lawn. He **watered** and **fertilized** his lawn quite often. His beautiful lawn now **had** growing problems. It **grew** too well because he **had** to mow it every week. That **was** his problem, right? Wrong! My dad **bought** sod for our "okay" yard. Right! I **had** to mow it!

Reference 58: Predicate Noun and Linking Verb

1. A **predicate noun** is a noun or pronoun after the verb that means the same thing as the subject.
2. A **predicate noun** is labeled as *PrN*. (Label a **predicate pronoun** as **PrP**.)
3. To find the **predicate noun**, ask WHAT or WHO after the verb.
4. A **predicate noun** is often called a predicate nominative.
5. A **predicate noun** always comes after a linking verb.
6. A **linking verb** links, or connects, the subject to a predicate noun or a predicate pronoun.

Example Sentence for the exact words to say to find the linking verb and predicate noun.

1. Dad is an excellent carpenter.
2. Who is an excellent carpenter? Dad - SN
3. What is being said about Dad? Dad is - V
4. Dad is what? carpenter - verify the noun
5. Does carpenter mean the same thing as Dad? Yes.
6. Carpenter - PrN *(Say: Carpenter - predicate noun.)*
7. Is - LV *(Say: Is - linking verb.)*
8. What kind of carpenter? excellent - Adj
9. An - A

10. SN LV PrN P4 Check *(Say: Subject Noun, Linking Verb, Predicate Noun, Pattern 4, Check.) (This first check is to make sure the "L" is added to the verb.)*
11. Linking verb - check again. *("Check again" means to check for prepositional phrases and then go through the rest of the Question and Answer Flow.)*
12. No prepositional phrases.
13. Period, statement, declarative sentence
14. Go back to the verb - divide the complete subject from the complete predicate.
15. Is there an adverb exception? No.
16. Is this sentence in a natural or inverted order? Natural - no change.

Reference 59: Contraction Chart			Pronoun	Contraction

AM

			HAS			**its**	**it's**
I am	–	I'm	has not	–	hasn't	(owns)	(it is)
			he has	–	he's	*its coat*	*it's cute*
IS			she has	–	she's		
is not	–	isn't					
he is	–	he's	**HAVE**				
she is	–	she's	have not	–	haven't	**your**	**you're**
it is	–	it's	I have	–	I've	(owns)	(you are)
who is	–	who's	you have	–	you've	*your car*	*you're right*
that is	–	that's	we have	–	we've		
what is	–	what's	they have	–	they've		
there is	–	there's				**their**	**they're**
			HAD			(owns)	(they are)
ARE			had not	–	hadn't	*their house*	*they're gone*
are not	–	aren't	I had	–	I'd		
you are	–	you're	he had	–	he'd		
we are	–	we're	she had	–	she'd	**whose**	**who's**
they are	–	they're	you had	–	you'd	(owns)	(who is)
			we had	–	we'd	*whose cat*	*who's going*
WAS, WERE			they had	–	they'd		
was not	–	wasn't					
were not	–	weren't	**WILL / SHALL**				
			will not	–	won't		
DO, DOES, DID			I will	–	I'll		
do not	–	don't	he will	–	he'll		
does not	–	doesn't	she will	–	she'll		
did not	–	didn't	you will	–	you'll		
			we will	–	we'll		
CAN			they will	–	they'll		
cannot	–	can't					
			WOULD				
LET			would not	–	wouldn't		
let us	–	let's	I would	–	I'd		
			he would	–	he'd		
			she would	–	she'd		
			you would	–	you'd		
			we would	–	we'd		
			they would	–	they'd		
			SHOULD, COULD				
			should not	–	shouldn't		
			could not	–	couldn't		

Reference 60: Degrees of Adjectives

The **Simple Form** is used when no comparison is made. There are no rules for the simple form. (**fast, nervous**)

The **Comparative Form** is used to compare **TWO** people, places, or things.

The **Superlative Form** is used to compare **THREE** or more people, places, or things.

Rule 1. Use *-er* with most 1 or 2 syllable words. (**faster**) Use *more* with *-ful* words or whenever the *-er* sounds awkward. (**more nervous**) Use *more* for all 3 or more syllable words.

Rule 2. Use *-est* with most 1 or 2 syllable words. (**fastest**) Use *most* with *-ful* words or whenever the *-est* sounds awkward. (**most nervous**) Use *most* for all 3 or more syllable words.

Irregular Adjectives Have No Rule Numbers and Have to be Memorized

Simple Adjective		Comparative		Superlative	
1. good	3. little (amount)	5. better	7. less or lesser	9. best	11. least
2. bad, ill	4. much, many	6. worse	8. more	10. worst	12. most

Sentence Examples

1. Thomas bought a good pen. 2. Thomas bought a better pen than Larry. 3. Thomas bought the best pen in the class.

Practice: Write the rule numbers and the different forms for the adjectives below. For irregular forms, write **Irr** in the box.

Simple Adjective Form	Rule Box	Comparative Adjective Form	Rule Box	Superlative Adjective Form
1. happy	1	happier	2	happiest
2. beautiful	1	more beautiful	2	most beautiful
3. bad	Irr	worse	Irr	worst

4. I am **taller** than Sam. (tall)　　5. Of all the girls, she was the **most eager** to go. (eager)　　6. She reads **better** than Sue. (good)

Reference 61: Double Negatives

Negative Words That Begin With *N*					Other Negative Words	Negative Prefixes
neither	no	no one	not (n't)	nowhere	barely, hardly, scarcely	dis, non, un
never	nobody	none	nothing			

Three Ways to Correct a Double Negative

Rule 1. **Change** the second negative to a positive:
　　Wrong: Debbie **couldn't** find **nothing**.　　Right: Debbie **couldn't** find **anything**.

Rule 2. **Take out** the negative part of a contraction:
　　Wrong: Debbie **couldn't** find **nothing**.　　Right: Debbie **could** find **nothing**.

Rule 3. **Remove** the first negative word (possibility of a verb change):
　　Wrong: Debbie **didn't** say **nothing**.　　Right: Debbie **said nothing**.

Changing Negative Words to Positive Words

1. Change *no* or *none* to *any*.
2. Change *nobody* to *anybody*.
3. Change *no one* to *anyone*.
4. Change *nothing* to *anything*.
5. Change *nowhere* to *anywhere*.
6. Change *never* to *ever*.
7. Change *neither* to *either*.
8. Remove the *n't* from a contraction.

Examples: Underline the negative words in each sentence. Rewrite each sentence and correct the double negative mistake as indicated by the rule number in parentheses at the end of the sentence.

1. He <u>doesn't</u> have <u>no</u> homework over the weekend. (Rule 3) **He has no homework over the weekend.**

2. I <u>can't</u> <u>hardly</u> wait for my birthday this year. (Rule 2) **I can hardly wait for my birthday this year.**

3. He <u>hasn't</u> done <u>nothing</u> about his problem. (Rule 1) **He hasn't done anything about his problem.**

Reference 62: Guidelines for Descriptive Writing

1. **When describing people,** it is helpful to notice these types of details: appearance, walk, voice, manner, gestures, personality traits, any special incident related to the person being described, and any striking details that will help make that person stand out in your mind.

2. **When describing places or things,** it is helpful to notice these types of details: the physical features of a place or thing (color, texture, smell, shape, size, age), any unusual features, any special incident related to the place or thing being described, and whether or not the place or thing is special to you.

3. **When describing nature,** it is helpful to notice these types of details: the special features of the season, the sights, smells, sounds, colors, animals, insects, birds, and any special incident related to the scene being described.

4. **When describing an incident or an event,** it is helpful to notice these types of details: the order in which the event takes place, any specific facts that will keep the story moving from a beginning to an ending, the answers to any of the *who, what, when, where, why,* and *how* questions that the reader needs to know, and especially the details that will create a clear picture, such as how things look, sound, smell, feel, etc.

Reference 63: Descriptive Paragraph Guidelines

A. Sentence 1 is the topic sentence that introduces **what is being described**.
B. For sentences 2-8, use **the descriptive details** in Reference 62.
C. Sentence 9 is a concluding sentence that **restates or relates back to the topic sentence**.

A Walk in the Woods

I always love to walk in the woods at my grandfather's farm. I like to spend time in his woods because it is full of surprises. This time, when I cross the ditch and squeeze under the barbed-wire fence, a small blue lizard startles me. I try to catch him, but he scurries under an old rotting log. The log has been lying there so long it has moss for a beard. Suddenly, I hear squeaky noises. As I look around, I spot a jay's nest on the limb above me, and over the side I can see four straggly little blue jays' heads. They are making squeaky noises, begging for one more grub or worm. As I walk in these woods, I am building memory treasures.

Reference 64: Personal Pronoun-Antecedent Agreement

   antecedent   pronoun   antecedent   pronoun
1. The *boy* loved *his* new computer.   2. The *boy* smiled. *He* had just bought a new computer.

1. Decide if the antecedent is singular or plural, and then choose the pronoun that agrees in number.

   If the antecedent is singular, the pronoun must be singular. (man - he, him, his, etc.)
   If the antecedent is plural, the pronoun must be plural. (men - they, them, their, etc.)

2. Decide if the antecedent is male or female, and then choose the pronoun that agrees in gender.

   If the antecedent is masculine, the pronoun must be masculine gender. (boy-he)
   If the antecedent is feminine, the pronoun must be feminine gender. (girl-she)
   If the antecedent is neither masculine or feminine, the pronoun must be neuter gender. (book-it)

   (The plural pronouns *they* and *them* also show neuter gender. The **trees** are dead. **They** burned in the fire.)

Reference 65: The Indefinite Pronouns

1. Singular Indefinite Pronouns

Singular indefinite subject pronouns take singular verbs. (**Everyone** in the class **wants** a ticket.) Once you learn the indefinite pronouns that are singular, choosing a singular verb is easy.

These indefinite pronouns will always be singular: those ending in **-one** (*anyone, everyone, someone, no one*) or **-body** (*anybody, everybody, somebody, nobody*) or **-thing** (*anything, everything, something*) and those that imply **one** or **none** (*one, each, either, neither, nothing, another*).

Singular indefinite pronouns used as antecedents must use singular personal pronouns for agreement in number. This is called singular pronoun-antecedent agreement. (**Everyone** should complete **his** assignment.) If the antecedent is a singular indefinite pronoun followed by a prepositional phrase, the object of a preposition may determine the gender, but it never determines the number of the personal pronoun chosen for agreement. (**Each** of the <u>women</u> was selected on the basis of <u>her</u> merit.)

2. Plural Indefinite Pronouns

Plural indefinite subject pronouns take plural verbs. (**Several** in the class **want** tickets.) Once you learn the indefinite pronouns that are plural, choosing a plural verb is easy.
These indefinite pronouns will always be plural: *both, few, many, others, several.*

Plural indefinite pronouns used as antecedents must use plural personal pronouns for agreement in number. This is called plural pronoun-antecedent agreement. (**Many** should complete **their** assignment.) If the antecedent is a plural indefinite pronoun followed by a prepositional phrase, the object of a preposition <u>does not</u> determine the gender or number of the personal pronoun chosen for agreement.

(**Several** of the <u>women</u> were selected on the basis of **their** merit.)

3. Indefinite Pronouns That Can Be Either Singular or Plural

Some indefinite pronouns can be **either singular or plural**: *all, most, none, some, any, half.*
If a prepositional phrase follows any of these indefinite pronouns, the object of the preposition determines whether the indefinite pronoun is singular or plural. <u>Singular</u>: Some (of the **trash**) **is** gone. <u>Plural</u>: Some (of the **gems**) **are** missing. If these indefinite pronouns are used alone, they are usually considered plural.

(**Some are** shivering from the cold.)

Remember, only the "either singular or plural" pronouns depend on prepositional phrases to determine whether they are singular or plural.

4. Antecedents of Indefinite Pronouns

The antecedent for every pronoun should be clear, and the pronoun should agree with its antecedent in both gender (male or female) and number (singular or plural). When gender is not specified, the general rule is to use the masculine form or rewrite the sentence.
(**Everyone** did **his** homework.) or (**Everyone** did the homework assigned.)

5. Ways Indefinite Pronouns Can Be Used

Indefinite pronouns can be used as subjects or objects, but if an indefinite word is used as an adjective, then it is not an indefinite pronoun.

<u>Subject</u>:   **Many** wait for the storm to pass.

<u>Object</u>:   The doctor helps **many** of the citizens.

<u>Adjective</u>: **Many** boys are in line.

Reference 66: Practice for Pronoun-Antecedent Agreement and Subject-Verb Agreement

For Parts 1 and 2, choose an answer from the choices in parentheses. Then, fill in the rest of the columns according to the titles. (**S** or **P** stands for singular or plural. **N/Pro** means to identify the subject as a noun or pronoun.)

Part 1: Pronoun-antecedent Agreement	Pronoun choice	S or P	Antecedent	S or P
1. The puppies barked hungrily at (its, their) mother.	their	P	puppies	P
2. The chairman was in (his, their) meeting.	his	S	chairman	S
3. Everyone needs (his, their) books today.	his	S	everyone	S

Part 2: Subject-verb Agreement	Subject	N/Pro	S or P	Verb choice
4. Everyone in town (yell, yells) at the games.	everyone	Pro	S	yells
5. Tom and Sam (love, loves) to fish.	Tom and Sam	N	P	love
6. Several cubs (is, are) searching for food.	cubs	N	P	are

Part 3: Identify these indefinite pronouns as singular (S), plural (P), or either (E) singular or plural.

__S__ 1. neither	__P__ 2. both	__S__ 3. nobody	__E__ 4. most	__S__ 5. everyone

Part 4: On notebook paper, write these indefinite pronouns: 17 singular indefinite pronouns (4/one, 4/body, 3/thing, 6/one or none), 5 plural indefinite pronouns, and 6 singular/plural indefinite pronouns.

Singular: one—anyone, everyone, someone, no one; **body**—anybody, everybody, somebody, nobody; **thing**—anything, everything, something; **one/none**—one, each, either, neither, nothing, another. **Plural:** both, few, many, others, several. **Sing/Plural:** all, most, none, some, any, half.

Reference 67: Sentence Pattern 5 and Predicate Adjective

1. A **predicate adjective** is an adjective after the verb that describes or tells what kind of subject.
2. A **predicate adjective** is labeled as **PA**.
3. To find the **predicate adjective**, ask WHAT KIND after the verb.
4. A **predicate adjective** always comes after a linking verb.
5. A **linking verb** links, or connects, the subject to a predicate adjective.

Sample Sentence for the exact words to say to find the linking verb and predicate adjective.

1. Her new dress is magnificent!
2. What is magnificent? dress - SN
3. What is being said about dress? dress is - V
4. Dress is what? magnificent - verify the adjective
5. What kind of dress? magnificent - PA
   (Say: Magnificent - predicate adjective.)
6. Is - LV
7. What kind of dress? new - Adj
8. Whose dress? her - PPA

9. SN LV PA P5 Check

   (Say: Subject Noun, Linking Verb, Predicate Adjective, Pattern 5, Check.) (This first check is to make sure the "L" is added to the verb.)

10. Linking verb - check again.

    ("Check again" means to check for prepositional phrases and then go through the rest of the Question and Answer Flow.)

11. No prepositional phrases.
12. Exclamation point. strong feeling, exclamatory sentence
13. Go back to the verb - divide the complete subject from the complete predicate.
14. Is there an adverb exception? No.
15. Is this sentence in a natural or inverted order? Natural - no change.

Reference 68: Rules for the Plurals of Nouns with Different Endings

1. "ch, sh, z, s, ss, x," add "es."	6. "f" or "ff," add "s."
2. a vowel plus "y," add an "s."	7. a vowel plus "o," add "s."
3. a consonant plus "y," change "y" to "i" and add "es."	8. a consonant plus "o," add "es."
4. "f" or "fe," change the "f" or "fe" to "v" and add "es."	9. stays the same for S and P.
5. irregular nouns-change spellings completely.	10. regular nouns, add "s."

Use the rules above to write the correct plural form of these nouns:

		Rule	Plural Form			Rule	Plural Form
1.	alley	2	alleys	2.	calf	4	calves
3.	roof	6	roofs	4.	deer	9	deer

Reference 69: The Five Parts of a Friendly Letter

1. Heading

1. Box or street address of writer
2. City, state, zip code of writer
3. Date letter was written
4. Placement: upper right-hand corner

2. Friendly Greeting or Salutation

1. Begins with *Dear*
2. Names person receiving the letter
3. Has comma after person's name
4. Placement: at left margin, two lines below heading

3. Body

1. Tells reason the letter was written
2. Can have one or more paragraphs
3. Has indented paragraphs
4. Is placed one line after the greeting
5. Skips one line between each paragraph

4. Closing

1. Closes letter with a personal phrase-(Your friend, With love,)
2. Capitalizes only first word
3. Is followed by a comma
4. Is placed two lines below the body
5. Begins just to the right of the middle of the letter

5. Signature

1. Tells who wrote the letter
2. Is usually signed in cursive
3. Uses first name only unless there is a question as to which friend or relative you are
4. Is placed beneath the closing

Friendly Letter Example

> **1. Heading**
> 1348 Grace St.
> Freeman, AR 71621
> June 6, 20__

2. Friendly Greeting, (or Salutation)

> Dear Carol,

3. Body (Indent Paragraphs)

> I'm glad to hear you are collecting dolls. I have over fifty in my collection. I will send you my favorite doll book. Take good care of it!

> **4. Closing,**
> Your aunt,

> **5. Signature**
> Aunt Joan

Reference 70: Envelope Parts	Friendly Envelope Example
The return address: 1. Name of the person writing the letter 2. Box or street address of the writer 3. City, state, zip code of the writer **The mailing address:** 1. Name of the person receiving the letter 2. Street address of the person receiving the letter 3. City, state, zip code of the person receiving the letter	**Return Address** Stamp Joan Bishop 1348 Grace St. Freeman, AR 71621 **Mailing Address** Carol Walker 5527 Smokey Lane Rock Hill, NM 11908

Reference 71: Four Types of Business Letters

Four common reasons to write business letters and information about the four types:

1. If you need to send for information - letter of inquiry.
2. If you want to order a product - letter of request or order.
3. If you want to express an opinion - letter to an editor or official.
4. If you want to complain about a product - letter of complaint.

Letter of Inquiry	Letter of Request or Order
1. Ask for information or answers to your questions. 2. Keep the letter short and to the point. 3. Word the letter so that there can be no question as to what it is you need to know.	1. Carefully and clearly describe the product. 2. Keep the letter short and to the point. 3. Include information on how and where the product should be shipped. 4. Include information on how you will pay for the product.

Letter to an Editor or Official	Letter of Complaint About a Product
1. Clearly explain the problem or situation. 2. Offer your opinion of the cause and possible solutions. 3. Support your opinions with facts and examples. 4. Suggest ways to change or improve the situation.	1. Carefully and clearly describe the product. 2. Describe the problem and what may have caused it. (Don't spend too much time explaining how unhappy you are.) 3. Explain any action you have already taken to solve the problem. 4. End your letter with the action you would like the company to take to solve the problem.

Reference 72: Business Letter Example

	1. HEADING
	313 West Drive
	Dover, Texas 12119
	May 22, 20__

2. INSIDE ADDRESS

Mr. Harold Dodd
Dusty's Air Services
2312 Barton Blvd.
Glen, Texas 98723

3. FORMAL GREETING, (OR SALUTATION)

Dear Mr. Dodd:

4. BODY (INDENT PARAGRAPHS)

I would like to have 200 acres of cotton sprayed for weeds. Please let me know what days you will be available in the next week.

5. FORMAL CLOSING,

Sincerely yours,

6. SIGNATURE

Tom Greene

Reference 73: Envelope Parts	Business Envelope Example

The return address:

1. Name of the person writing the letter
2. Box or street address of the writer
3. City, state zip code of the writer

The mailing address:

1. Name of the person receiving the letter
2. Name of the company receiving the letter
3. Street address of the person receiving the
4. City, state, zip code of the person
   receiving the letter

Return Address

Tom Greene
313 West Drive
Dover, Texas 12119

Stamp

Mailing Address

Mr. Harold Dodd, Pilot
Dusty's Air Services
2312 Barton Blvd.
Glen, Texas 98723

Reference 74: Thank-You Notes

For a Gift		For an Action	
What -	Thank you for... (tell color, kind, and item)	**What -**	Thank you for... (tell action)
Use -	Tell how the gift is used.	**Helped -**	Tell how the action helped.
Thanks -	I appreciate your remembering me with this special gift.	**Thanks -**	I appreciate your thinking of me at this time.

Example 1: Gift

608 Martin Street
Glennwood, Tennessee 46281
August 30, 20__

Dear Janet,

Thank you for the new Nancy Drew book. That makes 10 in my collection! I appreciate your thoughtful gift.

Your friend,
Jenny

Example 2: Action

456 Concord Street
East Plains, Maryland 60311
March 16, 20__

Dear John,

Thank you for helping with the Pick-Up-Litter Campaign. Our work was a huge success because of people like you. I appreciate your help very much.

Your friend,
Sam

Reference 75: Invitations

1.	**What**	– a farewell party
2.	**Who**	– for Terry Smith
3.	**Where**	– at 635 Ohio Circle
4.	**When**	– on Friday, July 14, at 2:00
5.	**Whipped Cream**	– We hope to see you there!

635 Ohio Circle
Randall, Montana 44629
July 14, 20__

Dear David,

You are invited to a farewell party for Terry Smith. He is moving to Texas. The party will be at 2:00 on Friday, July 14, in our backyard at 635 Ohio Circle. Lots of games and food are planned. We hope to see you there!

Your friends,
Sam and Stan Turner

Student Note: Notice that the five parts of an invitation are underlined in the example; however, you would not underline them in an actual invitation.

Reference 76: Parts of a [Book]

AT THE FRONT:

1. **Title Page.** This page has the full title of the book, th[e]
the name of the publishing company, and the city wh[ere]

2. **Copyright Page.** This page is right after the title [page]
was published and who owns the copyright. If the [ISBN (International
Standard Book Number), it is listed here.

3. **Preface** (also called **introduction**). If a book [has a preface, it will refer to the]
contents and will usually tell briefly why the b[ook was written.]

4. **Table of Contents.** This section lists the majo[r]
tells their page numbers.

5. **Body.** This is the main section, or text, of the book.

AT THE BACK:

6. **Appendix.** This section includes extra informative material such as maps, charts,
diagrams, letters, etc. It is always wise to find out what is in the appendix since it may [contain]
supplementary material that you could otherwise find only by going to the library.

7. **Glossary.** This section is like a dictionary and gives the meanings of some of the important
words in the book.

8. **Bibliography.** This section includes a list of books used by the author. It could serve as a
guide for further reading on a topic.

9. **Index.** This will probably be your most useful section. The purpose of the index is to help you
quickly locate information about the topics in the book. It has an alphabetical list of specific
topics and tells on which page that information can be found. It is similar to the table of
contents, but it is much more detailed.

Reference 77: Card Catalog Cards

Author Card	Title Card	Subject Card
586.3	586.3	586.3
Author-Pacton, James R.	Title Science for Kids and Parents	Topic Science Projects
Title Science for Kids and Parents	Author-Pacton, James R.	Author-Pacton, James R.
Ill. by Charles Finley	Ill. by Charles Finley	Title Science for Kids and Parents
Children's Press, Chicago	Children's Press, Chicago	Ill. by Charles Finley
(c1990) 116p.	(c1990) 116p.	Children's Press, Chicago
		(c1990) 116p.

Reference 78: Sample Index

L	O	T
Leashes, 23–25, 44	Obedience training,	Ticks, 37
	collars in, 23–24, 43; housebreaking, 25–26;	Training, *see* Obedience training.
	leashes in, 23–25, 44; for puppies, 23–24;	Tricks, 49–53
	simple commands, 45–48; special tricks, 49–53	

Reference 79: Sample Table of Contents

CONTENTS

Reference 80A: Outline Information

Outline Guide

Title

I. **Introduction**

II. **Main Topic** (First main point)
   A. **Subtopic** (Supports first main point)
     1. **Details** (Supports subtopic)
     2. **Details** (Supports subtopic)
   B. **Subtopic** (Supports first main point)
   C. **Subtopic** (Supports first main point)

III. **Main Topic** (Second main point)
   A. **Subtopic** (Supports second main point)
   B. **Subtopic** (Supports second main point)

IV. **Main Topic** (Third main point)
   A. **Subtopic** (Supports third main point)
   B. **Subtopic** (Supports third main point)

V. **Conclusion**

Sample Outline

Chores at Home

I. Introduction

II. Inside chores
   A. Keep bedroom clean
     1. Make bed
     2. Hang up clothes
   B. Empty trash
   C. Wash dishes

III. Outside chores
   A. Mow lawn
   B. Wash car

IV. Miscellaneous chores
   A. Clean garage
   B. Clean shed

V. Conclusion

Reference 80B: Outline Information

First, an outline has a TITLE.

- At first, your outline title should be the same or similar to your narrowed topic. This will help you stay focused on the main idea of your report. If you decide to change the title for your final paper, you must remember to change your outline title.

- Capitalizing rules for titles are the same for outlines as for final papers: Capitalize the first word, the last word, and all the important words in between them. Conjunctions, articles, and prepositions with fewer than five letters are not usually capitalized unless they are the first or last word. Titles for reports are not underlined or placed in quotation marks unless the title is a quotation.

Second, an outline has Roman numerals, called MAIN TOPICS.

- There must always be two or more Roman numerals. There can never be just one. For each Roman numeral, there is a paragraph. (Three Roman numerals - three paragraphs.)

- The information following a Roman numeral is called the main topic and gives the main idea, or main point, of each paragraph. It will be used to form the topic sentence of the paragraph.

- Every first word in a main topic is always capitalized.

- The periods after the Roman numerals must be lined up under each other.

Third, an outline has capital letters denoting SUBTOPICS.

- There must always be two or more capital letters. If you only have one, do not put it in the outline. Each capital letter is indented under the first word of the main topic.

- The information beside a capital letter is called the subtopic and gives details that support the main topic, or main point of the paragraph.

- Every first word in a subtopic is always capitalized.

- The periods after the capital letters must be lined up under each other.

Fourth, an outline sometimes has Arabic numerals, called DETAILS.

- There must always be two or more Arabic numerals. If you only have one, do not put it on the outline. Each Arabic numeral is indented under the first word of the subtopic.

- The information beside an Arabic numeral is called a detail and tells specific information about the subtopic of the paragraph.

- Every first word in a detail is always capitalized.

- The periods after the Arabic numerals must be lined up under each other.

Reference 81: Parallel Form for Outlines

Parallel Form

1. All the main topics in an outline should be in parallel form. This means that all the main topics should begin in the same way: all nouns, all verbs, all noun phrases, all verb phrases, all prepositional phrases, etc. If necessary, change or rearrange the words of your outline so they are parallel.

(I. Inside chores   II. Outside chores   III. Miscellaneous chores)
or
(I. My inside chores   II. My outside chores   III. My miscellaneous chores)

2. All the subtopics under Roman Numeral II must be in the same form. The subtopics under Roman numeral III must be in the same form, but Roman Numeral II subtopics do not have to be in the same form as Roman Numeral III subtopics, etc.

(A. Keep bedroom clean   B. Empty trash   C. Wash dishes)   (A. Mow lawn   B. Wash car)

3. All the details under Subtopic A must be in the same form. The details under Subtopic B must be in the same form, but Subtopic A details do not have to be in the same form as Subtopic B details.

(1. Make bed   2. Hang up clothes)

Reference 82: 13 Steps for Researching a Topic and Writing a Report

Step 1: Select a narrowed topic.

Step 2: Make a topic outline guide.

Step 3: Select sources by skimming.

Step 4: Make a bibliography card for each source selected.

Step 5: Take notes.

Step 6: Organize note cards.

Step 7: Write an outline.

Step 8: Write a rough draft.

Step 9: Edit the rough draft.

Step 10: Write the final outline.

Step 11: Write the final report.

Step 12: Put the final report and all related research work in the correct order.

Step 13: Hand in final report and all related papers.

(Note: Make sure you write everything except your final outline and report in pencil.)

Reference 83: (Step 1) Select a Narrowed Topic

Topic: Famous People

Narrowed Topic: Benjamin Franklin

Final narrowed topic: Benjamin Franklin's Accomplishments

Reference 84: (Step 2) Make a Topic and Main Point Outline Guide

Topic Categories for People

Automatic main points: Introduction / Conclusion

Choose 3 main points for the body of the report:

1. Childhood
2. Adult life
3. People or events that influenced his/her life
4. Accomplishments (may use up to three)
5. Characteristics (may describe up to three)
6. Unusual and interesting facts
7. Add another main point to fit your topic.

Topic Categories for Animals

Automatic main points: Introduction / Conclusion

Choose 3 main points for the body of the report:

1. Habitat (where it lives)
2. Physical characteristics (what it looks like)
3. What it eats and how it gets its food
4. Enemies
5. Unusual and interesting facts
6. Single animal or part of a group of animals?
7. Add another main point to fit your topic.

Topic Categories for Things

Automatic main points: Introduction / Conclusion

Choose 3 main points for the body of the report:

1. Location
2. Physical appearance, makeup, or identification (size, shape, looks, feel, weight, liquid, etc.)
3. Can it be classified into different groups?
4. Important behavior, characteristics, or use
5. Unusual and interesting facts
6. Does it change with time?
7. Add another main point to fit your topic.

Topic Categories for Places

Automatic main points: Introduction / Conclusion

Choose 3 main points for the body of the report:

1. Location
2. Is it real or imaginary?
3. Famous landmarks or physical characteristics (may use up to three)
4. Why is this place important or interesting?
5. What people and animals live there?
6. Major industries, products, and services
7. Add another main point to fit your topic.

Topic Categories for a Process

Automatic main points: Introduction / Conclusion

Choose 3 main points for the body of the report:

1. A process is how something is done or made.
2. Identify what the process is.
3. Identify why the process is necessary.
4. List the steps you must take in order to complete the project or process in the most logical order.
5. Add another main point to fit your topic.

Topic Categories for an Event

Automatic main points: Introduction / Conclusion

Choose 3 main points for the body of the report:

1. What was the event?
2. When and where did the event occur?
3. Reasons why the event occurred
4. Who or what was involved in the event?
5. What was the effect of the event?
6. Widespread importance of the event.
7. Add another main point to fit your topic.

Topic Categories for an Opinion, etc.

Automatic main points: Introduction / Conclusion

Main Points

1. First point and supporting sentences
2. Second point and supporting sentences
3. Third point and supporting sentences
4. Add another main point to fit your topic.

Topic Categories for Ideas, etc.

Automatic main points: Introduction / Conclusion

Main Points

1. Facts
2. Reasons
3. Examples
4. Add another main point to fit your topic.

Reference 85: (Step 3) Select Sources by Skimming

1. Skimming is reading only the key parts of a source to determine quickly if that source has information that will fit the narrowed topic and main points you have selected from the outline guide.

2. The key parts to skim are titles, topic headings in boldface type, first sentences of paragraphs, underlining, captions under pictures, text outlined by boxes, questions, and summaries.

3. The best way to skim several paragraphs in a longer article is to read all of the first paragraph because it usually contains a brief summary of the article. Then, read only the first sentence of each paragraph in the body of the article. This reading will give you a brief summary of each paragraph. Finally, read all of the last paragraph because it restates the most important points.

4. As you skim an article, consider these things: Does this information give enough facts about your narrowed topic and main points? Is the information interesting enough to use in your report? Is the information presented clearly, and is it easy to understand?

5. Skimming a source will quickly help you decide if the source can be used. If the source has enough information about your narrowed topic and main points, then it **can be used**. If the source does not have enough information about your narrowed topic and main points, then it **cannot be used**. If, after skimming several sources, you cannot find enough information about the original narrowed topic and main points, you need to go back to the Outline Guide for Topic Categories and Main Points and choose new main points. If you still cannot find enough information, you will need to choose another narrowed topic from your assignment sheet and select new main points for the new topic.

Reference 86: (Step 4) Make a Bibliography Card for Each Source Selected

Bibliography Card (Book)	Bibliography Card (Encyclopedia)
Underhill, Albert. <u>Famous Americans</u>. Chicago: Mountain Publishing, 1995.	Lee, Quincy. "Benjamin Franklin." <u>Coffman's Encyclopedia</u>. 1992 ed.

Reference 87: (Step 6) Organize Note Cards

1. Since you have written Introduction, Conclusion, and the three main points at the top of your note cards, most of your information is already organized.

2. Now, sort your note cards into piles according to the titles at the top of the note cards. (You should have five piles: the introduction, the three main points, and the conclusion.)

3. On the Introductory card(s), write **(Paragraph 1)** in parentheses after the title.

4. Next, arrange the cards with the main points in the order that you want to present them in your report.

5. Arrange the note cards within each main point in a logical order for your report.

6. For each main point, write **(Paragraph 2), (Paragraph 3),** or **(Paragraph 4)** in parentheses beside each title.

7. On the Conclusion card(s), write **(Paragraph 5)** in parentheses after the title.

8. Finally, number all your note cards in the upper right hand corner to prevent them from getting out of order. Put the bibliography card(s) at the end.

9. Put all cards in a Ziploc bag to be handed in with your final report.

Reference 88: (Step 5) Take Notes

1. Write the three main points that you selected from the topic category outline guide at the top of three note cards. (Make additional cards with the same titles if you need them.)

2. After you have decided on a source, **you must read the complete article** before you begin taking notes.

3. After you have read the article, begin taking notes on your note cards.

4. As you take your notes, start at the beginning of the article and work to the end.

5. As you work with each paragraph, select the note cards with the main points that match the information for that paragraph.

6. Take notes on each note card that supports the main points written on that note card. (Use the main points to be selective in your reading and note-taking.)

7. Summarize the information you put on your note cards in your own words. (Write your notes in phrases, not complete sentences, on the appropriate note card.)

8. Put only one note or closely-related notes on each note card.

9. Make sure each note taken is important for your reader to know.

10. Each note should be a supporting fact or detail about the main points at the top of each card.

11. If you use the exact words of a writer, put them in quotation marks.

12. At the bottom of every note card, write the title of the source and the page number you used.

13. Write the words **Introduction** and **Conclusion** at the top of two more note cards. (Your introduction note cards will be a little different from the note cards with main points.)

14. For the Introduction, look for interesting general information, definitions, or questions that are necessary to the general understanding of your paper or that would give extra information to make an interesting introduction.

15. For the Conclusion note cards, try to find several summarizing facts that support your introductory statements. Then, during your outlining stage, you will make your final note cards based on conclusions that you have drawn from your research.

Reference 89: Sample Note Cards

Introduction
contributed many things to colonial America during life
had many careers - printer, inventor, public servant

Coffman Encyclopedia, 1992, Vol. 6, p. 312

Inventor
invented heater stove (Franklin stove) that used less wood and produced more heat in room than fireplace
invented improved street light, bifocals
Coffman Encyclopedia, 1992, Vol. 6, p. 312

Printer
published Pennsylvania Gazette at age of 20
soon became best newspaper in colonies

Franklin wrote humorous articles - made it popular
Coffman Encyclopedia, 1992, Vol. 6, p. 312

Public Servant
established first hospital in colonies with Dr. Thomas Bond
established volunteer fire department, first library, postal system for colonies

Coffman Encyclopedia, 1992, Vol. 6, p. 312

Printer
published Poor Richard s Almanac
featured fictional character named Richard Saunders
contained moon phases, planting guide, Franklin s proverbs
Coffman Encyclopedia, 1994, Vol. 15, p. 98

Public Servant
served on committee to write the Declaration of Independence
served as ambassador to France to win support for colonies
   during Revolutionary war
Coffman Encyclopedia, 1992, Vol. 6, p. 312

Inventor
began inventing at age of 54 after retiring from printing
discovered electricity in lightning and invented lightning rod

Coffman Encyclopedia, 1994, Vol. 15, p. 98

Conclusion
one of greatest citizens of colonial American
contributions had great effect on America then and now

Coffman Encyclopedia, 1992, Vol. 6, p. 312

Reference 90: (Step 7) Write an Outline

To make an outline for your report, you must use the note cards that you have already organized. You must now transfer your notes from note cards to correct outline form. **Be aware that you may not use all of your notes as you make your outline.** You will then use your outline to write your report. (Remember to refer to the outline example in References 80A, 80B, and 81 to review punctuation and parallel form.)

1. **Title.** Write your outline title on the top line of your paper. It should be the same or similar to your narrowed topic.

2. **Main topics.** Look at the titles written at the top of each note card. They are **Introduction, Titles for three main points, and Conclusion.** These note-card titles will be the main topics of your outline. To write the main topics on your paper, put a Roman numeral beside each one, capitalize the first word, and skip several lines after each topic to give you room to write the rest of your outline. Roman numeral I. will be your first paragraph, Roman numeral II. will be your second paragraph, etc.

3. **Subtopics or details for the first main topic, the introduction.** Look at the notes on the note cards titled *Introduction.* You will write the notes that explain or support the introduction as subtopics A., B., C., etc. If any of your notes explain or support the subtopics, list them under that particular subtopic as 1., 2., etc.

4. **Subtopics or details for the second main topic, the first main point.** Look at the notes under the second main topic titled *Printer.* You will write the notes that explain or support the second main topic as subtopics A., B., C., etc. If any of your notes explain or support the subtopics, list them under that particular subtopic as 1., 2., etc.

5. **Subtopics or details for the third main topic, the second main point.** Look at the notes under the third main topic titled *Inventor.* You will write the notes that explain or support the third main topic as subtopics A., B., C., etc. If any of your notes explain or support the subtopics, list them under that particular subtopic as 1., 2., etc.

6. **Subtopics or details for the fourth main topic, the third main point.** Look at the notes under the fourth main topic titled *Public Servant.* You will write the notes that explain or support the fourth main topic as subtopics A., B., C., etc. If any of your notes explain or support the subtopics, list them under that particular subtopic as 1., 2., etc.

7. **Subtopics or details for the fifth main topic, the conclusion.** Look at the notes under the fifth main topic titled *Conclusion.* You will write the notes that explain or support the conclusion as subtopics A., B., C., etc. If any of your notes explain or support the subtopics, list them under that particular subtopic as 1., 2., etc.

Reference 91: Report Outline

The Accomplishments of Benjamin Franklin

I. Introduction
    A. Contributed many things to American society
    B. Had several careers in his life-time
    C. Was printer, inventor, and public servant
II. Printer
    A. Published <u>Pennsylvania Gazette</u> at age of 20
       1. Best newspaper in colonies
       2. Popular newspaper because of Franklin's humorous articles
    B. Published popular <u>Poor Richard's Almanac</u>
       1. Featured Richard Saunders
       2. Contained moon phases and a planting guide
       3. Included Franklin's proverbs and wise sayings from others
III. Inventor
    A. Began at age of 54 after retired from printing
    B. Discovered electricity in lightning and invented lightning rod
    C. Invented Franklin stove
       1. Used less wood
       2. Increased the heat in room
IV. Public servant
    A. Established first hospital, library, and post office
    B. Helped write <u>Declaration of Independence</u>
V. Conclusion
    A. One of the greatest citizens of colonial America
    B. Contributions still being felt in America today

Reference 92: (Step 8) Write a Rough Draft

1. Your report will be a five-paragraph report. You will have an introductory paragraph, three paragraphs in the body (a paragraph for each of the main points), and a concluding paragraph. Use a pencil, and skip every other line on your notebook paper.

2. **Paragraph 1: First Main Topic.** Look at the first main topic (Introduction) on your outline (Roman numeral I) and write at least three sentences for the introductory paragraph. The first sentence is a topic sentence that tells what your report is about. The second sentence is an extra information or definition sentence that tells more about the topic. The third sentence is an enumeration sentence that tells how many main points will be in the report.

3. **Paragraph 2: Second Main Topic.** Look at the second main topic (first main point) on your outline (Roman numeral II.) Write a topic sentence that states your second main topic and tells what this paragraph will be about. Remember to indent. Then, look at the subtopics and details on your outline and write complete sentences that support the main idea of this paragraph. Be sure to write the subtopic sentences and detail sentences in the order of your outline.

Reference 92: (Step 8) Write a Rough Draft (continued)

4. **Paragraph 3: Third Main Topic**. Look at the third main topic (second main point) on your outline (Roman numeral III). Write a topic sentence that states your third main topic and tells what this paragraph will be about. Remember to indent. Then, look at the subtopics and details on your outline and write complete sentences that support the main idea of this paragraph. Be sure to write the subtopic sentences and detail sentences in the order of your outline.

5. **Paragraph 4: Fourth Main Topic**. Look at the fourth main topic (third main point) on your outline (Roman numeral IV). Write a topic sentence that states your fourth main topic and tells what this paragraph will be about. Remember to indent. Then, look at the subtopics and details on your outline and write complete sentences that support the main idea of this paragraph. Be sure to write the subtopic sentences and detail sentences in the order of your outline.

6. **Paragraph 5: Fifth Main Topic**. Look at the fifth main topic (conclusion) on your outline (Roman numeral V). Then, look at the subtopics and details on your outline and write complete sentences that support the main idea of this paragraph. Be sure to write the subtopic sentences and detail sentences in the order of your outline. You should include summarizing sentences that restate or support the statements in your introduction. Your final sentence should be based on conclusions you have drawn from your research. Remember to indent.

7. **Title Page**. The title page will be the **first page** of your report. Make a title page with the following information: Skip three lines from the top line. On the fourth line, center the title of your report. Skip three more lines. On the next line, center "By (*your name*)." Skip three more lines. On the next line, center "(*your teacher's name*)." Under the teacher's name, on the next line, put the date.

8. **Bibliography Page**. At the end of your report, you will use your bibliography card(s) to list all the encyclopedias, books, and articles (sources) that you actually used in writing your paper. This bibliography page will be the **last page** of your report. On the top line, center "Bibliography Page," skip two lines, then copy the information on your bibliography cards to the notebook paper.

Reference 93: (Step 9) Edit a Rough Draft

Revision is part of writing. During the editing time, use Reference 38, the editing checklist, on page 29. Remember the rules of editing. You must edit your paper using each checkpoint. You should also remember to check for good organization, for clear and logical development of ideas, and for your general statements to be supported by details and examples. After you edit your rough draft, have at least one more person edit it. The final responsibility for editing, however, is yours. A quick review is provided below to help you do a final edit of your paper.

1. Is the first line of each paragraph indented?
2. Does your paper have an introduction, body, and conclusion?
3. Does each supporting sentence support the main idea sentence in each paragraph?
4. Do your main topics and supporting sentences follow the order of your outline?
5. Have you capitalized and punctuated your sentences correctly?
6. Have you spelled each word correctly?
7. Have you read your report orally to see how it sounds?
8. Have you checked for sentence fragments and run-on sentences?
9. Are your sentences varied to avoid monotony?
10. Have you completed a title page and a bibliography page and checked for correct form?

Reference 94: (Step 10) Write the Final Outline

Check over your rough draft outline to see if there are any revisions necessary after writing and editing the rough draft of your report. Make any necessary changes. Then, write your final outline neatly in ink. Both outlines will be handed in with your final report.

Reference 95: (Step 11) Write the Final Report

Before you recopy your edited rough draft for your final paper, re-read the introductory and concluding paragraphs. Your introduction should get the reader s interest and should briefly tell the main idea of the report. Your conclusion should restate your most important points. Make any necessary changes. Also, decide if you want to include illustrations with your final report. If so, they must be completed at this point. Then, write your final report neatly in ink. Finally, proofread your final paper again.

Reference 96: Final Report Example

The Accomplishments of Benjamin Franklin

Benjamin Franklin contributed many things to American society. Because he was extremely intelligent and hard-working, Franklin had several careers in his lifetime. Three of these careers were printer, inventor, and public servant.

Benjamin Franklin s first career was as a printer. At the age of 20, Franklin began publishing the *Pennsylvania Gazette*. This newspaper soon became the best newspaper in the colonies because of Franklin s humorous articles. Franklin also had great success publishing the *Poor Richard s Almanac*. It featured a fictional character named Richard Saunders and contained moon phases, a planting guide, and his now-famous proverbs.

Franklin s second career started at the age of 54 when he began to invent practical things to help himself and others. One of his inventions, the lightning rod, was made after his discovery that electricity was present in lightning. Another invention, the Franklin stove, used less wood and produced better heat in homes than the fireplace.

His third career, as a public servant, was accomplished throughout his adult life. As a young man, Franklin was instrumental in establishing the first hospital, the first library, and the first post office in colonial America. Later in his life, Franklin was one of the major writers of the <u>Declaration of Independence</u>.

In conclusion, Benjamin Franklin was truly one of the greatest citizens of colonial America. The impact of his contributions as a printer, an inventor, and a public servant are still being felt in America today.

Reference 97: (Step 12) Put the Final Report and All Related Research Papers in the Correct Order

1. Title page - in ink
2. Final report - in ink
3. Illustrations (optional)
4. Bibliography page - in ink
5. Final outline - in ink
6. Rough draft - in pencil
7. Rough draft outline - in pencil
8. Note cards and bibliography cards (Put all cards in a Ziploc bag.)

Reference 98: (Step 13) Hand in Final Report and All Related Papers
Make sure all papers are in order and ready to be handed in. Then, hand in your report and all related papers when your teacher calls for them.

Reference 99: Report Topics for Writing Assignment #49		
1. Countries **(Any country of your choice)**	2. Famous People Famous Scientists/Inventors **(Marie Curie, Albert Einstein, or any scientist or inventor of your choice)**	3. Musical Instruments Woodwinds, Brass, or Percussion **(Any woodwind, brass, or percussion instrument of your choice)**
4. Animals Snakes **(Any snake of your choice)**	5. Famous Americans Presidents **(Any American president of your choice)**	6. Sports Team Sports **(Baseball, football, basketball, soccer, hockey, volleyball, etc.)**

PRACTICE

SECTION

Chapter 1, Lesson 5, Practice

Exercise 1: Identify each pair of words as synonyms or antonyms by putting parentheses **( )** around **syn** or **ant**. For number 5, write two synonym words and identify them with **syn**. For number 6, write two antonym words and identify them with **ant**.

1. disprove, attest	syn ant	3. defer, postpone	syn ant	5.
2. commodities, goods	syn ant	4. astute, obtuse	syn ant	6.

Chapter 2, Lesson 3, Practice 1

Put the end mark and the abbreviation for each kind of sentence in the blanks below.

1. Sit down when you tie your shoe laces _____

2. Did you do well on your exam _____

3. He won every race _____

4. I'm leaving on my trip tomorrow _____

Chapter 2, Lesson 3, Practice 2

On notebook paper, write a sentence to demonstrate each of these four kinds of sentences:
(1) Declarative (2) Interrogative (3) Exclamatory (4) Imperative. Write the correct punctuation and the abbreviation that identifies it at the end. Use these abbreviations: **D, Int, E, Imp**.

Chapter 2, Lesson 3, Practice 3

Match the definitions. Write the correct letter beside each numbered concept.

_____ 1. exclamatory sentence	A. verb, adjective, or adverb
_____ 2. a/an are also called	B. who
_____ 3. adjective modifies	C. what is being said about
_____ 4. verb question	D. person, place, thing, or idea
_____ 5. a definite article	E. what
_____ 6. subject-noun question (thing)	F. period
_____ 7. article adjective can be called	G. shows strong feeling
_____ 8. makes a request or gives a command	H. indefinite articles
_____ 9. noun	I. noun or pronoun
_____ 10. subject-noun question (person)	J. the
_____ 11. punctuation for declarative	K. noun marker
_____ 12. adverb modifies	L. imperative sentence

Chapter 2, Lesson 3, Practice 4

Write the answer for each question.

1.   What are the three article adjectives?   _____

2.   What word tells what the subject does?   _____

Chapter 3, Lesson 1, Practice

Underline the complete subject once and the complete predicate twice in the sentence below. Then, complete the table below.

_____   The   damaged   truck   drove   slowly   away.

List the Noun Used	List the Noun Job	Singular or Plural	Common or Proper	Simple Subject	Simple Predicate

Chapter 3, Lesson 2, Practice

Underline the complete subject once and the complete predicate twice in the sentence below. Then, complete the table below.

_____   The   injured   wolf   limped   slowly   away.

List the Noun Used	List the Noun Job	Singular or Plural	Common or Proper	Simple Subject	Simple Predicate

Finding One Part of Speech: For each sentence, write **SN** above the simple subject and **V** above the simple predicate. Underline the word(s) for the part of speech listed to the left of each sentence.

Adjective(s):   1. The   cold,   white   snow   fell   silently   today.

Adverb(s):   2. The   beautiful   white   swan   finally   flew   very   gracefully   away.

Noun(s):   3. The   head   football   coach   left   early   yesterday.

Adjective(s):   4. The   copperhead   quickly   crawled   away.

Verb(s):   5. The   soccer   team   played   extremely   well.

Chapter 3, Lesson 3, Practice

Put this 3-part assignment on notebook paper: (1) Write the four parts of speech that you have studied so far (in any order). (2) Write out the Question and Answer Flow in exact order for the sentence listed below. (3) Classify the sentence.

Practice Sentence: The   small   frugal   woman   shopped   wisely.

Chapter 3, Lesson 5, Practice

Use this three-point outline form to guide you as you write a three-point expository paragraph.

Write a topic: _____

Write 3 points to enumerate (list) specifics about the topic.

1. _____   2. _____   3. _____

Sentence #1 Topic sentence (*Use words in the topic and tell how many points will be used.*)

_____

Sentence #2 3-point sentence (*List your 3 points in the order that you will present them.*)

_____

Sentence #3 State your first point in a complete sentence.

_____

Sentence #4 Write a supporting sentence for the first point.

_____

Sentence #5 State your second point in a complete sentence.

_____

Sentence #6 Write a supporting sentence for the second point.

_____

Sentence #7 State your third point in a complete sentence.

_____

Sentence #8 Write a supporting sentence for the third point.

_____

Sentence #9 Concluding sentence (*Restate the topic sentence and add an extra thought.*)

_____

Student Note: Rewrite your nine-sentence paragraph on notebook paper. Be sure to indent and use the checklists to help you edit your paragraph. Make sure you re-read your paragraph several times slowly.

Chapter 4, Lesson 3, Practice 1

Rule 1: A singular subject must use a singular verb form that ends in **s**: *is, was, has, does, or verbs ending with* **es**.
Rule 2: A plural subject, a compound subject, or the subject **YOU** must use a plural verb form that has **no s** ending: *are, were, do, have, or verbs without* **s** *or* **es** *endings.* (A plural verb form is also called the *plain form*.)

Examples: For each sentence, do these four things: (1) Write the subject. (2) Write **S** if the subject is singular or **P** if the subject is plural. (3) Write the rule number. (4) Underline the correct verb in the sentence.

Subject	S or P	Rule	
			1. The girls (was, were) talking in the classroom.
			2. Sam and Jerry (is, are) good runners.
			3. Our truck (was, were) sliding on the snow covered road.

Chapter 4, Lesson 3, Practice 2

On notebook paper, write a Practice and Improved Sentence, using these labels:

A   Adj   Adj   SN   V   Adv   Adv

Chapter 4, Lesson 3, Practice 3

Put this 3-part assignment on notebook paper: (1) Write the four parts of speech that you have studied so far (in any order). (2) Write out the Question and Answer Flow in exact order for the sentence listed. (3) Classify the sentence.

Practice Sentence: Slowly,   the   unsteady   vagrant   staggered   away.

Chapter 5, Lesson 3, Practice 1

Write the five parts of speech that you have studied so far (in any order) on notebook paper.

Chapter 5, Lesson 3, Practice 2

Choose one set of labels below and write Practice and Improved Sentences on notebook paper.

A Adv Adj SN V Adv P A Adj OP   or   **A Adj Adj SN P A OP V Adv P A Adj OP**

Chapter 6, Lesson 1, Practice 1

Write the five parts of speech that you have studied so far (in any order) on notebook paper.

Chapter 6, Lesson 1, Practice 2

Choose one set of labels below and write Practice and Improved Sentences on notebook paper.

A Adv Adj SN V Adv P A Adj OP P A OP   or   **A Adj SN P A OP V P A Adj OP P A OP**

Chapter 10, Lesson 3, Practice

Use the Editing Guide below each sentence to know how many capitalization and punctuation errors to correct. For Sentence 1, write the capitalization and punctuation rule numbers for each correction in bold. For Sentence 2, write the capitalization and punctuation corrections. Use the capitalization and punctuation rule pages to help you.

1. **W**ell, **I'**ll go to **G**alveston, **T**exas, in **J**une for the annual sales meeting with **J**ohn **C**ross, my boss.

Editing Guide for Example 1 Sentence: Capitals: 7   Commas: 4   Apostrophes: 1   End Marks: 1

2. will barrette tonys new puppy be trained by henry to be an elite european show dog

Editing Guide for Example 2 Sentence: Capitals: 5   Commas: 2   Apostrophes: 1   End Marks: 1

Chapter 11, Lesson 1, Practice

Write the capitalization and punctuation rule numbers for each correction in bold.

700 **S**outh **M**iami **A**ve.

Cleveland, **O**hio 60001

May 28, 20—

Dear **S**usie,

I have a surprise for you. **A** huge celebration is planned for the **F**ourth of **J**uly. **T**he **C**leveland players will dress like **G**eorge **W**ashington. **P**layers on the opposing team will dress like **A**braham **L**incoln. **I**ndependence **D**ay at the ballpark should be an entertaining afternoon.

I hope you can come to **O**hio in **J**uly to visit. **W**rite soon.

Your cousin,

Rachel

Editing Guide: Capitals: 27   Commas: 4   Periods: 1   End Marks: 7

Chapter 11, Lesson 2, Practice

Write the capitalization and punctuation corrections only.

7005 shamrock lane

lincoln nebraska 55556

march 27 20—

dear aunt loretta

i can hardly believe you and lucy are going with the school band to the indiana state fair this

year i hear the competition is fierce we all wish you the best of luck let me know how you did

your only nephew

timothy

| Editing Guide: | Capitals: 18 | Commas: 4 | End Marks: 4 |

Chapter 12, Lesson 3, Practice

Make corrections to the following paragraph.

Football and basketball is sports that have many things in common the most obvious similaries are

the retangular playing area a ball and two teams. Both sports is team sports, and winning depends

on every member of the team working together as one unit. Both sports have an offence to score

points and a defence to keep the other team from scoring. Finally, both sports has cheerleaders

and widespread support of fans

Total Mistakes: 13

Chapter 13, Lesson 1, Practice 1

On notebook paper, add the part that is underlined in the parentheses to make each fragment into a complete sentences.

1. Under the porch in the backyard
   (subject part, predicate part, <u>both the subject and predicate</u>)

2. Screeched and squealed on the concrete
   (<u>subject part</u>, predicate part, both the subject and predicate)

3. The soft white feather from the baby owl
   (subject part, <u>predicate part</u>, both the subject and predicate)

Chapter 13, Lesson 1, Practice 2

Identify each kind of sentences by writing the abbreviation in the blank. (**S, F**).

_____ 1. The choir sang sweetly.

_____ 2. In the water.

_____ 3. Geese flew.

_____ 4. Leaving the stadium.

_____ 5. The huge rocks.

Chapter 13, Lesson 2, Practice 1

Put a slash to separate each run-on sentences below. Then, correct the run-on sentences by rewriting them as indicated by the labels in parentheses at the end of each sentence.

1. The little children were sleeping they were tired. (**SS**)

_____

2. The garden hose is in the garage the lawnmower is in the garage. (**SCS**)

_____

3. The dog jumped up it leapt through the hoop. (**SCV**)

_____

Chapter 13, Lesson 2, Practice 2

Identify each kind of sentence by writing the abbreviation in the blank. (**S, SS, F, SCS, SCV**)

_____ 1. After the pie was eaten.

_____ 2. Our dog chewed the shoe and scattered it everywhere.

_____ 3. Green and gold are our team colors.

_____ 4. The bulb was not working. Dad changed it.

_____ 5. The goose settled down on her nest of eggs.

Chapter 13, Lesson 3, Practice 1

Put a slash to separate each run-on sentence below. Then, correct the run-on sentences by rewriting them as indicated by the labels in parentheses at the end of each sentence.

1. The unhappy boy pleaded with his mother she still said no. (**CD**, but)

_____

_____

2. The unhappy boy pleaded with his mother she still said no. (**CD**; however,)

_____

_____

3. The unhappy boy begged his mother he pleaded with his mother. (**SCV**)

_____

_____

4. The unhappy boy pleaded with his mother she still said no. (**CD**;)

_____

_____

Chapter 13, Lesson 3, Practice 2 and 3	
Chapter 13, Lesson 3, Practice 2:	Chapter 13, Lesson 3, Practice 3:
Identify each kind of sentence by writing the abbreviation in the blank. (**S, F, SCS, SCV, CD**)	Write three compound sentences on notebook paper using these labels to guide you:
_____1. The boy ran and jumped across the fence.	① (**CD**, but)
_____2. Dad watched television; Mom read a book.	② (**CD**; therefore,)
_____3. Our dog and cat smelled the meat cooking.	③ (**CD**;)
_____4. Crammed into the crowded elevator.	

Chapter 14, Lesson 1, Practice 1

Put a slash to separate each run-on sentence below. Then, correct the run-on sentences by rewriting them as indicated by the labels in parentheses **( )** at the end of each sentence.

1. Mother turned the key the car started. (CX, when) (1)

_____

_____

2. Mother turned the key the car started. (CX, until) (2)

_____

_____

Chapter 14, Lesson 1, Practice 2

Identify each kind of sentence by writing the abbreviation in the blank. (**S, F, SCS, SCV, CD, CX**)

_____ 1. You left your bicycle out in the rain; consequently, it rusted.

_____ 2. During the musical, Jan and Joe sang a duet.

_____ 3. During the summer when the games were over.

_____ 4. When I heard the noise, I ran to the window.

_____ 5. During the musical, Jan sang and danced.

_____ 6. The ice melted after the sun came out.

Chapter 14, Lesson 2, Practice 1

Put a slash to separate each run-on sentence below. Then, correct the run-on sentences by rewriting them as indicated by the labels in parentheses ( ) at the end of each sentence.

---

1. Mother turned the key the car would not start. (**CX**, even though) (1)

_____

_____

2. The sun rose again the farmers were busy with chores. (**CX**, before) (1)

_____

_____

3. The little boy smiled the clown gave him a balloon. (**CX**, after) (2)

_____

_____

Chapter 14, Lesson 2, Practice 2

Identify each kind of sentence by writing the abbreviation in the blank. (**S, F, SCS, SCV, CD, CX**)

_____ 1. Because Jean's stories were funny.

_____ 2. The electrician and plumber arrived at the same time.

_____ 3. I heard the noise and ran to the window.

_____ 4. I heard the noise; therefore, I ran to the window.

_____ 5. I ran to the window because I heard the noise.

_____ 6. I heard the noise, and I ran to the window.

_____ 7. Because I heard the noise, I ran to the window.

Chapter 14, Lesson 2, Practice 3

On notebook paper, write three complex sentences. Underline each <u>subordinate</u> sentence.

Chapter 14, Lesson 3, Practice 1

Put a slash to separate each run-on sentence below. Then, correct the run-on sentences by rewriting them as indicated by the labels in parentheses ( ) at the end of each sentence.

1. The   wind   blew   hard   it   did   not   rain   or   storm. (**CX**, although) (1)

_____

_____

2. The   family   shelled   peas   Mom   cooked   dinner. (**CX**, while) (2)

_____

_____

Chapter 14, Lesson 3, Practice 2

Identify each kind of sentence by writing the abbreviation in the blank. (**S, F, SCS, SCV, CD, CX**)

_____1. We laughed during the funny movie.

_____ 2. My brother and sister came home for Christmas.

_____ 3. The clowns played music and sang to the children.

_____ 4. The cold freezing rain in the winter.

_____ 5. I did my homework, but I left it at home.

Chapter 14, Lesson 3, Practice 3

On notebook paper, write three complex sentences. Underline each <u>subordinate</u> sentence.

Chapter 14, Lesson 3, Practice 4

On notebook paper, write a compound sentence for each of these labels:

① (**CD**, but)
② (**CD**; therefore,)
③ (**CD**;)

Chapter 15, Lesson 1, Practice

Part A: Underline each noun to be made possessive and write singular or plural (**S-P**), the rule number, and the possessive form. Part B: Write each noun as singular possessive and then as plural possessive.

1. For a singular noun - add (**'s**) **Rule 1: boy's**			2. For a plural noun that ends in **s** - add (**'**) **Rule 2: boys'**	3. For a plural noun that does not end in **s** - add (**'s**) **Rule 3: men's**		
Part A	**S-P**	**Rule**	**Possessive Form**	**Part B**	**Singular Poss**	**Plural Poss**
1. dog bone				5. boy		
2. children voices				6. man		
3. Smiths phones				7. giraffe		
4. monkeys cages				8. secretary		

Chapter 15, Lesson 2, Practice

Part A: Underline each noun to be made possessive and write singular or plural (**S-P**), the rule number, and the possessive form. Part B: Write each noun as singular possessive and then as plural possessive.

1. For a singular noun - add (**'s**) **Rule 1: boy's**			2. For a plural noun that ends in **s** - add (**'**) **Rule 2: boys'**	3. For a plural noun that does not end in **s** - add (**'s**) **Rule 3: men's**		
Part A	**S-P**	**Rule**	**Possessive Form**	**Part B**	**Singular Poss**	**Plural Poss**
1. Thomas foot				5. child		
2. agent gun				6. book		
3. Denise letter				7. wife		
4. cats paws				8. son		

Chapter 15, Lesson 3, Practice

Part A: Underline each noun to be made possessive and write singular or plural (**S-P**), the rule number, and the possessive form. Part B: Write each noun as singular possessive and then as plural possessive.

1. For a singular noun - add (**'s**) **Rule 1: boy's**			2. For a plural noun that ends in **s** - add (**'**) **Rule 2: boys'**	3. For a plural noun that does not end in **s** - add (**'s**) **Rule 3: men's**		
Part A	**S-P**	**Rule**	**Possessive Form**	**Part B**	**Singular Poss**	**Plural Poss**
1. tractor tires				5. wolf		
2. Gus friend				6. mouse		
3. truck bumpers				7. ax		
4. women dresses				8. child		

Chapter 16, Lesson 3, Practice

For Sentences 1-4, replace each underlined pronoun by writing the correct form in the first blank and **S** or **O** for subjective or objective case in the second blank.

1. <u>Us</u> boys heard a terrible explosion. _____ _____

2. Take a ticket from <u>we</u> girls. _____ _____

3. Reserve a table for Dad and <u>we</u>. _____ _____

4. Tom and <u>them</u> will likely be late. _____ _____

Chapter 17, Lesson 1, Practice

Use the Quotation Rules to help punctuate the quotations below. Underline the explanatory words.

1. senator   edwards   insisted   the   time   has   come   for   campaign   reform

2. the   time   has   come   for   campaign   reform   senator   edwards   insisted

3. i   yelled   to   susie   before   the   easter   ceremony   don't   forget   the   flowers

4. don't   forget   the   flowers   i   yelled   to   susie   before   the   easter   ceremony

Chapter 17, Lesson 2, Practice 1

Use the Quotation Rules to help punctuate the quotations below. Underline the explanatory words.

1. mom   said   kimberly   i   want   you   to   do   the   dishes   tonight

2. kimberly   i   want   you   to   do   the   dishes   tonight   mom   said

3. kimberly   mom   said   i   want   you   to   do   the   dishes   tonight

Chapter 17, Lesson 2, Practice 1 (continued)

4. kimberly i want you to do the dishes tonight said mom i have a meeting after supper i wont get back in time to do them

5. will you aunt sarah asked close the door daniel

6. will you close the door daniel asked aunt sarah uncle thomas is cold could you also take this letter to the mailbox

Chapter 17, Lesson 2, Practice 2

On notebook paper, write three sentences, demonstrating each of the three quotations: Beginning quote, end quote, and split quote.

Chapter 17, Lesson 3, Practice 1

Use the Quotation Rules to help punctuate the quotations below. Underline the explanatory words.

1. elizabeth do you want to go to the movies tonight asked timothy

2. timothy asked elizabeth do you want to go to the movies tonight

3. elizabeth timothy asked do you want to go to the movies tonight

4. elizabeth do you want to go to the movies tonight asked timothy a really good movie is showing downtown at seven

Chapter 17, Lesson 3, Practice 2

On notebook paper, write three sentences, demonstrating each of the three quotations: Beginning quote, end quote, and split quote.

Chapter 18, Lesson 1, Practice

Underline each verb or verb phrase. Identify the verb tense by writing a number **1** for present tense, a number **2** for past tense, or a number **3** for future tense. Write the past tense form and **R** or **I** for Regular or Irregular.

Verb Tense		Main Verb Past Tense Form	R or I
	1. My sister swims every weekend.		
	2. We had laughed at his funny jokes.		
	3. We are laughing at his funny jokes.		
	4. We laugh at his funny jokes.		
	5. The small boy ran after the bus.		
	6. Were you painting your house?		
	7. My parents have gone to town.		

Chapter 18, Lesson 2, Practice

Underline each verb or verb phrase. Identify the verb tense by writing a number **1** for present tense, a number **2** for past tense, or a number **3** for future tense. Write the past tense form and **R** or **I** for Regular or Irregular.

Verb Tense		Main Verb Past Tense Form	R or I
	1. The boys are building the fence.		
	2. Did you eat the peaches?		
	3. The pitcher has thrown the catcher the ball.		
	4. I am washing the dog.		
	5. I will be leaving soon.		
	6. Two birds fly to the big oak tree in our yard.		
	7. We have walked a mile.		
	8. The fireworks will begin at eight o'clock.		
	9. They were running to the bus.		

Chapter 18, Lesson 3, Practice 1

Underline each verb or verb phrase. Identify the verb tense by writing a number **1** for present tense, a number **2** for past tense, or a number **3** for future tense. Write the past tense form and **R** or **I** for Regular or Irregular.

Verb Tense		Main Verb Past Tense Form	R or I
	1. The boys are building the fence.		
	2. Did you eat the peaches?		
	3. I will be leaving soon.		
	4. We have walked a mile.		

Chapter 18, Lesson 3, Practice 2

Change the underlined present tense verbs in Paragraph 1 to past tense verbs in Paragraph 2.

Paragraph 1: Present Tense

The door on the old house **creaks** open. A sinister face **appears** behind the window. A black cat **dashes** across our feet, and we **scream** loudly. We **fly** down the rickety steps and across the overgrown lawn. Our hearts **pound**, and we **slip** through a hole in the fence. Then, we **turn** and **see** my big brother. He **stands** on the porch of the old house with a Halloween mask in his hand. He **laughs** at the joke on us!

Paragraph 2: Past Tense

The door on the old house _____ open. A sinister face _____ behind the window. A black cat _____ across our feet, and we _____ loudly. We _____ down the rickety steps and across the overgrown lawn. Our hearts _____, and we _____ through a hole in the fence. Then, we _____ and _____ my big brother. He _____ on the porch of the old house with a Halloween mask in his hand. He _____ at the joke on us!

Chapter 18, Lesson 3, Practice 3

Write the seven present tense helping verbs, the five past tense helping verbs, and the two future tense helping verbs.

Present Tense Helping Verbs	Past Tense Helping Verbs	Future Tense Helping Verbs
_____	_____	_____
_____	_____	_____
_____	_____	
_____	_____	
_____	_____	
_____		
_____		

Chapter 18, Lesson 3, Practice 4

Change the underlined mixed tense verbs in Paragraph 1 to present tense verbs in Paragraph 2.

Paragraph 1: Mixed Tenses

Every day, I **swim** in our pool at my house. I **had learned** to swim five lengths of our pool. It **was** fun. My six-year-old sister **is** not afraid to swim, either. She **jumped** off the side of the pool into the water and **swims** to the other side. My sister and I **were** good swimmers, but we still **needed** swimming lessons. I **took** advanced swimming lessons now, and my sister **takes** intermediate swimming lessons. We **had** a good instructor, and he **taught** us a lot of new things.

Paragraph 2: Present Tense

Every day, I _____ in our pool at my house. I _____ _____ to swim five lengths of our pool. It _____ fun. My six-year-old sister _____ not afraid to swim, either. She _____ off the side of the pool into the water and _____ to the other side. My sister and I _____ good swimmers, but we still _____ swimming lessons. I _____ advanced swimming lessons now, and my sister _____ intermediate swimming lessons. We _____ a good instructor, and he _____ us a lot of new things.

Chapter 19, Lesson 3, Practice

Copy the following words on notebook paper. Write the correct contraction beside each word.

Words: cannot, let us, do not, was not, they are, are not, had not, is not, she is, who is, you are, did not, it is, we are, were not, does not, has not, I am, I have, I had, will not, I will, would not, I would, should not, could not, they would.

Chapter 20, Lesson 1, Practice 1

Write the rule numbers and the different forms for the adjectives below. For irregular forms write **Irr**.

Comparative: Rule 1: Use **-er** with 1 or 2 syllable words and **more** with -ful words, awkward words, or words with 3 or more syllables.
Superlative: Rule 2: Use **-est** with 1 or 2 syllable words and **most** with -ful words, awkward words, or words with 3 or more syllables.

Simple Adjective Form	Rule Box	Comparative Adjective Form	Rule Box	Superlative Adjective Form
1. good				
2. comfortable				
3. funny				
4. helpful				
5. fine				
6. dependable				
7. bad				

Chapter 20, Lesson 1, Practice 2

In each blank, write the correct form of the adjective in parentheses to complete the sentences.

1. Juan has completed the _____ part of his training. (difficult)

2. This gold is _____ than the gold in that necklace. (fine)

3. Kelly was a very _____ assistant for the program. (helpful)

4. The chocolate cookies were _____ than the sugar cookies. (good)

5. Of all the stories, yours is _____. (good)

Chapter 20, Lesson 2, Practice 1

Underline the negative words in each sentence. Rewrite each sentence and correct the double negative mistake as indicated by the rule number in parentheses at the end of the sentence.

Rule 1	Rule 2	Rule 3
Change the second negative to a positive.	Take out the negative part of a contraction.	Remove the first negative word (verb change).

1. She couldn't find nothing in her desk. (Rule 2)

2. He doesn't have no money. (Rule 3)

3. They don't know nothing about it. (Rule 1)

4. We couldn't get no supplies today. (Rule 1)

5. Doug hadn't never played basketball. (Rule 2)

6. There wasn't no time left. (Rule 1)

7. Don't never miss Ms. Blue's class. (Rule 1)

8. I didn't find no key. (Rule 3)

Chapter 20, Lesson 2, Practice 2

On notebook paper, make a list of fifteen contractions, then write the words from which the contractions come.

Chapter 20, Lesson 3, Practice 1

Underline the negative words in each sentence. Rewrite each sentence and correct the double negative mistake as indicated by the rule number in parentheses at the end of the sentence.

Rule 1	Rule 2	Rule 3
Change the second negative to a positive.	Take out the negative part of a contraction.	Remove the first negative word (verb change).

1. She didn't ask no questions today. (Rule 3)

5. She couldn't find nothing in her purse. (Rule 2)

2. We didn't get no sleep last night. (Rule 1)

6. He couldn't see nothing without his glasses. (Rule 1)

3. I haven't never camped out. (Rule 2)

7. I didn't believe no one. (Rule 1)

4. He doesn't never wear a coat. (Rule 3)

8. He wasn't never late. (Rule 2)

Chapter 20, Lesson 3, Practice 2

On notebook paper, write three sentences in which you demonstrate each of the double negative rules. Underline the negative word in each sentence.

Chapter 20, Lesson 3, Practice 3

Write the rule numbers and the different forms for the adjectives below. For irregular forms, write **Irr**.

Comparative: Rule 1: Use **-er** with 1 or 2 syllable words and **more** with -ful words, awkward words, or words with 3 or more syllables.
Superlative: Rule 2: Use **-est** with 1 or 2 syllable words and **most** with -ful words, awkward words, or words with 3 or more syllables.

Simple Adjective Form	Rule Box	Comparative Adjective Form	Rule Box	Superlative Adjective Form
1. gentle				
2. little				
3. honorable				
4. green				
5. fair				
6. many				
7. playful				

Chapter 20, Lesson 3, Practice 4

On notebook paper, write three sentences, demonstrating each of the three degrees of adjectives. Identify the form you used by writing **simple, comparative, or superlative** at the end of each sentence.

Chapter 20, Lesson 3, Practice 5

In each blank, write the correct form of the adjective in parentheses to complete the sentences.

1. Jamie is the _____ member of the class. (listless)

2. This was the _____ cole slaw I'd ever eaten. (good)

3. Krystal was a very _____ assistant for the program. (persnickety)

4. Tristan had the _____ handwriting in the class. (legible)

5. Toby greeted strangers in a very _____ manner. (formal)

Chapter 20, Lesson 3, Practice 6

On notebook paper, make a list of ten contractions, then write the words from which the contractions come.

Chapter 21, Lesson 1, Practice 1

Parts 1 and 2: Choose an answer from the choices in parentheses. Fill in the other columns according to the titles. (**S** or **P** stands for singular or plural. **N/Pro** means to identify the subject as a noun or pronoun.)

Part 1: Pronoun-antecedent agreement

Pronoun Choice	S or P	Antecedent	S or P

1. The nurses checked (her, their) patients.

2. Dad had chicken for (his, their) birthday.

3. Everybody heard (his, their) own name called.

4. Anyone can buy (his, their) own football jacket.

5. Several ate (his, their) lunches in the park.

Part 2: Subject-verb Agreement

Subject	N/Pro	S or P	Verb choice

6. Either of the two choices (is, are) fine.

7. Two sacks of money (was, were) found in the car.

8. A sack of money (was, were) found in the car.

9. Everything (don't, doesn't) go up to the attic.

10. All of the band members (feel, feels) proud.

Chapter 21, Lesson 1, Practice 2

Identify the indefinite pronouns as singular (**S**), plural (**P**), or either (**E**) singular or plural.

_____ 1. nobody _____ 2. some _____ 3. each _____ 4. few _____ 5. everyone

Chapter 21, Lesson 1, Practice 3

On notebook paper, write these indefinite pronouns: 17 singular indefinite pronouns (4/one, 4/body, 3/thing, 6/one or none), 5 plural indefinite pronouns, and 6 singular/plural indefinite pronouns.

Chapter 21, Lesson 2, Practice 1

Parts 1 and 2: Choose an answer from the choices in parentheses. Fill in the other columns according to the titles. (**S** or **P** stands for singular or plural. **N/Pro** means to identify the subject as a noun or pronoun.)

Part 1: Pronoun-antecedent agreement

1. The leader of the troops lost (his, their) voice.

2. The mailboxes had no names on (it, them).

3. Each of the cadets raised (his, their) right hand.

4. The chickens laid (its, their) eggs in the morning.

Pronoun Choice	S or P	Antecedent	S or P

Part 2: Subject-verb Agreement

5. Everyone in the bleachers (was, were) hysterical.

6. Two bows on the package (is, are) adequate.

7. The seashells on the beach (has, have) cracks.

8. Nothing in the refrigerator (is, are) spoiled.

Subject	N/Pro	S or P	Verb choice

Chapter 21, Lesson 2, Practice 2

Identify the indefinite pronouns as singular (**S**), plural (**P**), or either (**E**) singular or plural.

_____ 1. everyone _____ 2. any _____ 3. several _____ 4. anybody _____ 5. something

Chapter 21, Lesson 2, Practice 3

On notebook paper, write these indefinite pronouns: 17 singular indefinite pronouns (4/one, 4/body, 3/thing, 6/one or none), 5 plural indefinite pronouns, and 6 singular/plural indefinite pronouns.

Chapter 21, Lesson 3, Practice 1

Parts 1 and 2: Choose an answer from the choices in parentheses. Fill in the other columns according to the titles. (**S** or **P** stands for singular or plural. **N/Pro** means to identify the subject as a noun or pronoun.)

Part 1: Pronoun-antecedent agreement

1. The dogs in the park had lost (its, their) collars.

2. Something in the bushes got (its, their) foot stuck.

3. The fans got (its, their) own way this time.

4. Everything has (its, their) own special place.

Pronoun Choice	S or P	Antecedent	S or P

Part 2: Subject-verb Agreement

5. One of the candles (is, are) broken.

6. The flight from Dallas (was, were) two hours late.

7. Many of the tourists (feel, feels) betrayed.

8. Neither of the answers (was, were) correct.

Subject	N/Pro	S or P	Verb choice

Chapter 21, Lesson 3, Practice 2

Identify the indefinite pronouns as singular (**S**), plural (**P**), or either (**E**) singular or plural.

_____ 1. half   _____ 2. both   _____ 3. no one   _____ 4. each   _____ 5. nobody

Chapter 21, Lesson 3, Practice 3

On notebook paper, write these indefinite pronouns: 17 singular indefinite pronouns (4/one, 4/body, 3/thing, 6/one or none), 5 plural indefinite pronouns, and 6 singular/plural indefinite pronouns.

Chapter 22, Lesson 3, Practice 1

Write the rule number from Reference 68 and the correct plural form of the nouns below.

		Rule	Plural Form
1.	alley		
2.	calf		
3.	roof		
4.	deer		
5.	child		

		Rule	Plural Form
6.	box		
7.	radio		
8.	tomato		
9.	cat		
10.	try		

Chapter 22, Lesson 3, Practice 2

On notebook paper, make a list of ten contractions, then write the words from which the contractions come.

Chapter 22, Lesson 3, Practice 3

On notebook paper, write three sentences, demonstrating each of the three quotations. Underline the explanatory words.

Chapter 23, Lesson 1, Practice

Use butcher paper, large pieces of construction paper, or poster board to make a colorful wall poster to identify the five parts of a friendly letter and the parts of an envelope. Write the title and an example for each of the five parts. Illustrate your work. Then, give an oral presentation about the friendly letter and the envelope when you have finished.

Chapter 23, Lesson 2, Practice

Write a friendly letter to a special friend or relative. Before you start, review the references and tips for writing friendly letters. After your letter has been edited, fold the letter and put it in an envelope. Address the envelope properly and mail it. Don't forget the stamp. (*E-mail does not take the place of this assignment.*)

Chapter 23, Lesson 3, Practice 1

On notebook paper, identify the parts of a friendly letter and envelope by writing the titles and an example for each title. (*Use References 69 and 70 to check the parts of a friendly letter and envelope.*)

Chapter 23, Lesson 3, Practice 2

Write a friendly letter to a neighbor, nursing home resident, or relative. This person must be someone that is different from the person chosen in the previous lesson. Before you start, review the references and tips for writing friendly letters. After your letter has been edited, fold the letter and put it in an envelope. Address the envelope properly and mail it. Don't forget the stamp.

Chapter 24, Lesson 1, Practice

Use butcher paper, large pieces of construction paper, or poster board to make a colorful wall poster to identify the six parts of a business letter and the parts of a business envelope. Write the title and an example for each of the parts of the business letter and envelope. Illustrate your work. Then, give an oral presentation about the business letter and the envelope when you have finished.

Chapter 24, Lesson 2, Practice

Write a friendly letter to a special friend or relative. Before you start, review the references and tips for writing friendly letters. After your letter has been edited, fold the letter and put it in an envelope. Address the envelope properly and mail it. Don't forget the stamp.

Chapter 24, Lesson 3, Practice 1

On notebook paper, identify the parts of a business letter and envelope by writing the titles and an example for each title. (*Use References 72 and 73 to check the parts of a business letter and envelope.*)

Chapter 24, Lesson 3, Practice 2

Write a business letter. You may invent another company and the situation for which you are writing. Before you begin, review the reasons for writing business letters and the four types of business letters (Reference 71 on page 46). After your letter has been edited, fold the letter and put it in an envelope. Address the envelope properly.

Chapter 25, Lesson 1, Practice

Write your own thank-you note. First, think of a person who has done something nice for you or has given you a gift (*even the gift of time*). Next, write that person a thank-you note, using the information in the Reference section as a guide.

Chapter 25, Lesson 2, Practice

Make your own invitation card. First, think of a special event or occasion and who will be invited. Next, make an invitation to send out. Use the information in the Reference section as a guide. Illustrate your card appropriately.

Chapter 25, Lesson 3, Practice 1

Write another thank-you note. First, think of a person who has done something nice for you or has given you a gift (*even the gift of time*). Next, write that person a thank-you note, using the information in the Reference section as a guide.

Chapter 25, Lesson 3, Practice 2

Make another invitation card. First, think of a special event or occasion and who will be invited. Next, make an invitation to send out, using the information in the Reference section as a guide. Illustrate your card appropriately.

Chapter 26, Lesson 2, Practice 1

Match each part of a book listed below with the type of information it may give you. Write the appropriate letter in the blank. You may use each letter only once.

A. Title Page   B. Copyright Page   C. Index   D. Bibliography   E. Appendix   F. Glossary

1. _____ A list of books used by the author as references

2. _____ ISBN number

3. _____ Used to locate topics quickly

Chapter 26, Lesson 2, Practice 2

Match each part of a book listed below with the type of information it may give you. Write the appropriate letter in the blank. You may use each letter only once.

A. Title Page	B. Table of Contents	C. Copyright Page	D. Index	E. Bibliography
F. Preface	G. Body			

1. _____ Exact page numbers for a particular topic

2. _____ Text of the book

3. _____ Reason the book was written

4. _____ Books listed for finding more information

Chapter 26, Lesson 2, Practice 3

On notebook paper, write the five parts found at the front of a book.

Chapter 26, Lesson 2, Practice 4

On notebook paper, write the four parts found at the back of a book.

Chapter 26, Lesson 3, Practice

Write the nine parts of a book on a poster and write a description beside each part. Illustrate and color the nine parts.

Chapter 27, Lesson 1, Practice 1
Underline or write the correct answer.

1. Biographies and autobiographies are arranged on the shelves in

   (**numerical order**   **alphabetical order**).

2. The main reference book that is primarily a book of maps is the

   (**encyclopedia**   **dictionary**   **atlas**   **almanac**).

3. The main reference book that is published once a year with a variety of up-to-date information is the

   (**encyclopedia**   **dictionary**   **atlas**   **almanac**).

4. What would you find by going to *The Readers' Guide to Periodical Literature*?

   _____

5. What are the names of the three types of cards located in the card catalog?

   _____

Chapter 27, Lesson 1, Practice 2
Write True or False after each statement.

1. The title of the book is always the first line on each of the catalog cards. _____

2. The *Readers' Guide to Periodical Literature* is an index to magazines. _____

3. Biographies are arranged on the shelves according to the author's last name. _____

4. The books in the nonfiction section are arranged numerically by a call number. _____

5. Fiction and nonfiction books have numbers on their spines to locate them on a shelf. _____

Chapter 27, Lesson 1, Practice 3

Draw and label the three catalog cards for this book on a sheet of notebook paper: 812.4 *Poetry in Modern America* by Harvey Collier, Paradise Press, Miami, 1994, 203 p. *(Use the catalog card examples in Reference 77.)*

Chapter 27, Lesson 1, Practice 4

Select eight of your favorite fiction books and alphabetize them by the authors' last names.

Chapter 27, Lesson 2, Practice

Using the index of a science (*or other subject*) book, write ten things that the index could help you answer quickly, and the pages where the answers are found.

Chapter 27, Lesson 3, Practice

Answer the questions below about the table of contents.

1. What is the title of the chapter that would tell you what to do if you need to know how often to feed your dog?

2. What is the number of the chapter?

3. On which page does Chapter 3 begin?

4. On which page does Chapter 3 end?

Chapter 28, Lesson 1, Practice

Give an oral report on parallel forms for outlines. Make an outline as a visual aid to help in your presentation. You may use the discussion points on parallel forms that are listed below. (*You may use Reference 81 as your guide.*)

1. Explain that parallel form means using the same type of words to start each division of your outline.

2. Discuss how you can start each section with all nouns, all verbs, all prepositions, adjectives in front of nouns, etc.

3. Discuss how you used parallel form in each section of your outline.

4. Each new section can have a different parallel form. Explain that it doesn't matter how each section begins, it is just important to make sure each section has the same parallel form.

Chapter 28, Lesson 2, Practice

Copy the notes below into a two-point outline. Change wording to put notes into correct parallel form.

Notes	Outline
time at the bus stop	
things to do	
respect other people's property	
be considerate of the rights of others	
what not to do	
don't wake the neighborhood	
shove and push other kids	

Chapter 28, Lesson 3, Practice

Copy the notes below into a two-point outline. Change wording to put notes into correct parallel form.

Notes	Outline
cleaning-up the kitchen	
before washing the dirty dishes	
scraping the plates	
rinse the silverware	
after the dishes are washed	
let them drain	
dry them	
putting them away	

TEST

SECTION

Chapter 2 Test

Exercise 1: Put the end marks and the abbreviations for each kind of sentence in the blanks below.

1. Did you vote in the election   _____

2. My uncle bought a new car   _____

3. I lost my new job   _____

4. Turn the heat on low   _____

5. Did Jimmy get to work on time   _____

6. I typed my resume on the computer   _____

7. Close the garage door   _____

8. The desperate mother screamed for help   _____

Exercise 2: On notebook paper, write a sentence to demonstrate each of these four kinds of sentences: (1) Declarative (2) Interrogative (3) Exclamatory (4) Imperative. Write the correct punctuation and the abbreviation that identifies it at the end. Use these abbreviations: **D, Int, E, Imp.** (Answers will vary.)

Exercise 3: Match the definitions. Write the correct letter beside each numbered concept.

_____ 1. tells what the subject does	A.	verb, adjective, or adverb
_____ 2. a/an are also called	B.	what?
_____ 3. adjective modifies	C.	what is being said about?
_____ 4. verb question	D.	person, place, or thing
_____ 5. a definite article	E.	indefinite articles
_____ 6. subject-noun question (thing)	F.	period
_____ 7. article adjective can be called	G.	noun marker
_____ 8. makes a request or gives a command	H.	who?
_____ 9. noun	I.	noun or pronoun
_____ 10. subject-noun question (person)	J.	the
_____ 11. punctuation for declarative	K.	verb
_____ 12. adverb modifies	L.	imperative sentence

Exercise 4: Identify each pair of words as synonyms or antonyms by putting parentheses ( ) around *syn* or *ant*.

1. gargantuan, diminutive	syn ant	3. germinate, stagnate	syn ant
2. loquacious, garrulous	syn ant	4. exuberant, flamboyant	syn ant

Exercise 5: Write a pair of synonyms beside number 1. Write a pair of antonyms beside number 2.

1. _____   2. _____

Exercise 6: In your journal, write a paragraph summarizing what you have learned this week.

Chapter 3 Test

Exercise 1: Classify each sentence.

1. _____ The   three   little   handsome   kangaroos   jumped   playfully.

2. _____ The   big,   ugly   mosquito   quickly   flew   away.

3. _____ The   eleven   football   players   turned   swiftly   around.

Exercise 2: Use Sentence 3 to underline the complete subject once and the complete predicate twice and to complete the table below.

List the Noun Used	List the Noun Job	Singular or Plural	Common or Proper	Simple Subject	Simple Predicate
1.	2.	3.	4.	5.	6.

Exercise 3: Name the four parts of speech that you have studied so far.

1. _____ 2. _____ 3. _____ 4. _____

Exercise 4: Finding One Part of Speech. For each sentence, write **SN** above the simple subject and **V** above the simple predicate. Underline the word(s) for the part of speech listed to the left of each sentence.

Adjective(s):   1. The   big   red   ball   bounced   rapidly   away.

Adverb(s):   2. The   brook   merrily   gurgled   swiftly   along.

Noun(s):   3. The   bluebird   flew   away.

Adjective(s):   4. The   monkeys   chattered   wildly.

Verb(s):   5. The   class   behaved   very   well.

Adverb(s):   6. The   colorful   clown   smiled   sadly   today.

Exercise 5: Identify each pair of words as synonyms or antonyms by putting parentheses ( ) around **syn** or **ant**.

1. defer, postpone	syn ant	5. bereavement, loss	syn ant	9. predicament, dilemma	syn ant
2. astute, obtuse	syn ant	6. gargantuan, diminutive	syn ant	10. commodities, goods	syn ant
3. loquacious, garrulous	syn ant	7. germinate, stagnate	syn ant	11. endorse, denounce	syn ant
4. exuberant, flamboyant	syn ant	8. tribulation, ecstasy	syn ant	12. disprove, attest	syn ant

Exercise 6: In your journal, write a paragraph summarizing what you have learned this week.

Chapter 4 Test

Exercise 1: Classify each sentence.

1. _____ Sometimes, an old wool sweater fits rather snugly.

2. _____ The unusually windy speaker surprisingly stopped quite abruptly.

3. _____ The young ministerial student walked confidently away.

Exercise 2: Use Sentence 2 to underline the complete subject once and the complete predicate twice and to complete the table below.

List the Noun Used	List the Noun Job	Singular or Plural	Common or Proper	Simple Subject	Simple Predicate
1.	2.	3.	4.	5.	6.

Exercise 3: Name the four parts of speech that you have studied so far.

1. _____ 2. _____ 3. _____ 4. _____

Exercise 4: For each sentence, write the subject, then write **S** if the subject is singular or **P** if the subject is plural, write the rule number, and underline the correct verb in the sentence.

Rule 1: A singular subject must use a singular verb form that ends in **s**: *is, was, has, does, or verbs ending with **s** or **es***.
Rule 2: A plural subject, a compound subject, or the subject **YOU** must use a plural verb form that has **no s** ending: *are, were, do, have, or verbs without **s** or **es** endings*. (A plural verb form is also called the *plain form*.)

Subject	S or P	Rule

1. The kites (has, have) long tails.
2. This skateboard (roll, rolls) great on the street.
3. The trucks in the parking lot (is, are) red.
4. The motorcycle (run, runs) smoothly on premium gas.
5. You (is, are) doing that all wrong.
6. They (was, were) fishing for catfish all night.
7. He (calls, call) my house every day.
8. The girls (was, were) caught in the rainstorm.
9. Ben and Jerry (is, are) good boys.
10. (Was, Were) your friends with you today?
11. Our truck (was, were) sliding on the wet road.
12. (Do, Does) the football players run every day?

Exercise 5: Identify each pair of words as synonyms or antonyms by putting parentheses ( ) around **syn** or **ant**.

1. defer, postpone	syn ant	5. complicated, intricate	syn ant	9. bereavement, loss	syn ant
2. astute, obtuse	syn ant	6. disprove, attest	syn ant	10. exuberant, flamboyant	syn ant
3. obfuscate, confuse	syn ant	7. loquacious, garrulous	syn ant	11. gargantuan, diminutive	syn ant
4. commodities, goods	syn ant	8. preposterous, reasonable	syn ant	12. deplorable, admirable	syn ant

Exercise 6: In your journal, write a paragraph summarizing what you have learned this week.

Chapter 5 Test

Exercise 1: Classify each sentence.

1. _____ During the night, the raccoons prowled inside the garbage cans.

2. _____ The striped salamander quickly darted under a rotten log.

3. _____ Three brave rescuers plunged bravely into the cold water!

Exercise 2: Use Sentence 3 to underline the complete subject once and the complete predicate twice and to complete the table below.

List the Noun Used	List the Noun Job	Singular or Plural	Common or Proper	Simple Subject	Simple Predicate
1.	2.	3.	4.	5.	6.
7.	8.	9.	10.		

Exercise 3: Name the five parts of speech that you have studied so far.

1. _____ 2. _____ 3. _____ 4. _____ 5. _____

Exercise 4: Identify each pair of words as synonyms or antonyms by putting parentheses ( ) around **syn** or **ant**.

1. benevolent, charitable	syn ant	5. obfuscate, confuse	syn ant	9. bereavement, loss	syn ant
2. frugal, extravagant	syn ant	6. methodical, chaotic	syn ant	10. exuberant, flamboyant	syn ant
3. contingency, serendipity	syn ant	7. complicated, intricate	syn ant	11. loquacious, garrulous	syn ant
4. predicament, dilemma	syn ant	8. preposterous, reasonable	syn ant	12. deplorable, admirable	syn ant

Exercise 5: For each sentence, write the subject, then write **S** if the subject is singular or **P** if the subject is plural, write the rule number, and underline the correct verb in the sentence.

Rule 1: A singular subject must use a singular verb form that ends in **s**: *is, was, has, does, or verbs ending with **s** or **es***.
Rule 2: A plural subject, a compound subject, or the subject **YOU** must use a plural verb form that has **no s** ending: *are, were, do, have, or verbs without **s** or **es** endings*. (A plural verb form is also called the *plain form*.)

Subject	S or P	Rule

1. Alice and Joe (vote, votes) faithfully every year.
2. The ice cream (was, were) melting in the hot car.
3. My friend (does, do) volunteer work at the city shelter.
4. Our puppies (was, were) playing in the pond.
5. My house (look, looks) like it's made to last.
6. Your hat and coat (is, are) on my bed.
7. The bird (was, were) pecking the cow.
8. (Was, Were) your friends with you yesterday?
9. Jason and Paul (is, are) going to the store.
10. The newborn baby (has, have) small feet.

Exercise 6: In your journal, write a paragraph summarizing what you have learned this week.

Chapter 6 Test

Exercise 1: Classify each sentence.

1. _____ He drove carefully across our bridge during the winter storm.

2. _____ We prayed constantly for our sick friend.

3. _____ Ease very gently into the cold water.

Exercise 2: Use Sentence 1 to underline the complete subject once and the complete predicate twice and to complete the table below.

List the Noun Used	List the Noun Job	Singular or Plural	Common or Proper	Simple Subject	Simple Predicate
1.	2.	3.	4.	5.	6.
7.	8.	9.	10.		

Exercise 3: Name the six parts of speech that you have studied so far.

1. _____   2. _____   3. _____   4. _____   5. _____   6. _____

Exercise 4: Identify each pair of words as synonyms or antonyms by putting parentheses ( ) around **syn** or **ant**.

1. obfuscate, confuse	syn ant	5. congenial, compatible	syn ant	9. contingency, serendipity	syn ant
2. deplorable, admirable	syn ant	6. defer, postpone	syn ant	10. complicated, intricate	syn ant
3. travail, labor	syn ant	7. commodities, goods	syn ant	11. loquacious, garrulous	syn ant
4. frugal, extravagant	syn ant	8. tribulation, ecstasy	syn ant	12. benevolent, charitable	syn ant

Exercise 5: For each sentence, write the subject, then write **S** if the subject is singular or **P** if the subject is plural, write the rule number, and underline the correct verb in the sentence.

Rule 1: A singular subject must use a singular verb form that ends in **s**: *is, was, has, does, or verbs ending with **s** or **es***.
Rule 2: A plural subject, a compound subject, or the subject **YOU** must use a plural verb form that has **no s** ending: *are, were, do, have, or verbs without **s** or **es** endings*. (A plural verb form is also called the *plain form*.)

Subject	S or P	Rule

1. My teeth (was, were) in excellent condition.
2. Susan and Jan (is, are) driving to Memphis.
3. The flowers (has, have) many blooms left.
4. This garden (need, needs) watering everyday.
5. The stairs (is, are) very steep at the mall.
6. My student (was, were) taken to the school nurse.
7. Hamburgers (is, are) my favorite meal.
8. (Do, Does) these pens have red ink in them?
9. The party (appear, appears) to be a success.
10. The cook (was, were) in a hurry to leave after lunch.

Exercise 6: On notebook paper, write as many prepositions as you can.

Exercise 7: In your journal, write a paragraph summarizing what you have learned this week.

Chapter 7 Test

Exercise 1: Classify each sentence.

1. _____ Yesterday, the sheriff's deputy fired directly over the rioters' heads!

2. _____ During band practice, we rehearsed endlessly for our upcoming band competition.

3. _____ The parishioners gathered at the edge of the river for the baptismal service.

Exercise 2: Use Sentence 1 to underline the complete subject once and the complete predicate twice and to complete the table below.

List the Noun Used	List the Noun Job	Singular or Plural	Common or Proper	Simple Subject	Simple Predicate
1.	2.	3.	4.	5.	6.
7.	8.	9.	10.		

Exercise 3: Name the six parts of speech that you have studied so far.

1. _____ 2. _____ 3. _____ 4. _____ 5. _____ 6. _____

Exercise 4: Identify each pair of words as synonyms or antonyms by putting parentheses ( ) around **syn** or **ant**.

1. contingency, serendipity	syn ant	4. docile, aggressive	syn ant	7. travail, labor	syn ant
2. beseech, entreat	syn ant	5. ambiguous, obvious	syn ant	8. swoon, revive	syn ant
3. lavish, sumptuous	syn ant	6. melancholy, felicitous	syn ant	9. congenial, compatible	syn ant

Exercise 5: Finding One Part of Speech. For each sentence, write **SN** or **SP** above the simple subject and **V** above the simple predicate. Underline the word(s) for the part of speech listed to the left of each sentence.

Adjective(s): 1. Several football players traveled in my uncle's chartered bus.

Preposition(s): 2. I usually live in Australia during the winter.

Pronoun(s): 3. My friends and I yelled at our friends from my brother's new car.

Exercise 6: For each sentence, write the subject, then write **S** if the subject is singular or **P** if the subject is plural, write the rule number (Rule 1 for singular and Rule 2 for plural), and underline the correct verb in the sentence.

Subject	S or P	Rule

1. These azaleas (grow, grows) quite well in a shaded area.
2. Susan and Jan (is, are) going to the state roundup.
3. The boa constrictor (was, were) in its cage.
4. You (was, were) a hero in the eyes of our students!
5. (Doesn't, Don't) your sister drive an antique Hudson?
6. (Do, Does) the band members get free tickets to the fair?
7. My shoes in the hall closet (was, were) muddy.
8. (Has, Have) Toni and her friends been to the lake?

Exercise 7: On a sheet of paper, write seven subject pronouns, seven possessive pronouns, and seven object pronouns.

Exercise 8: In your journal, write a paragraph summarizing what you have learned this week.

Chapter 8 Test

Exercise 1: Classify each sentence.

1. _____ Did the tiny green hummingbird dart quickly from the bird feeder?

2. _____ Several celebrities in the parking lot could be seen from our plane.

3. _____ The three extremely talented interns have not returned from their assignments.

Exercise 2: Use Sentence 2 to underline the complete subject once and the complete predicate twice and to complete the table below.

List the Noun Used	List the Noun Job	Singular or Plural	Common or Proper	Simple Subject	Simple Predicate
1.	2.	3.	4.	5.	6.
7.	8.	9.	10.		
11.	12.	13.	14.		

Exercise 3: Name the six parts of speech that you have studied so far.

1. _____ 2. _____ 3. _____ 4. _____ 5. _____ 6. _____

Exercise 4: For each sentence, write the subject, then write **S** if the subject is singular or **P** if the subject is plural, write the rule number (Rule 1 for singular and Rule 2 for plural), and underline the correct verb in the sentence.

Subject	S or P	Rule

1. You (laugh, laughs) like my dad.
2. Ribbons (was, were) tied to the trees in her yard.
3. (Do, Does) the papers belong on the floor?
4. My books (was, were) in the back seat of the car.
5. The nurse (is, are) getting the shot ready.
6. You (wasn't, weren't) late to band practice.
7. Keith and Josh (has, have) eaten all of the lasagna.

Exercise 5: Finding One Part of Speech. For each sentence, write **SN** above the simple subject and **V** (or **HV** and **V**) above the simple predicate. Underline the word(s) for the part of speech listed to the left of each sentence.

Preposition(s): 1. The opposing teams from local schools gathered for the final game of the season.

Verb(s): 2. During the summer, we are flying to Europe for our vacation.

Pronoun(s): 3. I am not traveling to Canada with my friends.

Exercise 6: Identify each pair of words as synonyms or antonyms by putting parentheses ( ) around **syn** or **ant**.

1. endorse, denounce	syn ant	5. surmise, guess	syn ant	9. entreat, beseech	syn ant
2. collate, sort	syn ant	6. felicitous, melancholy	syn ant	10. congenial, compatible	syn ant
3. obvious, ambiguous	syn ant	7. benevolent, charitable	syn ant	11. germinate, stagnate	syn ant
4. preposterous, reasonable	syn ant	8. terminate, initiate	syn ant	12. frugal, extravagant	syn ant

Exercise 7: In your journal, write a paragraph summarizing what you have learned this week.

Chapter 9 Test

Exercise 1: Classify each sentence.

1. _____ The algebra teacher and his student practiced with several new problems.

2. _____ Do not fish in the polluted waters of the large lake behind our house.

3. _____ Did the bright red cardinal chirp loudly during the early morning hours?

Exercise 2: Use Sentence 2 to underline the complete subject once and the complete predicate twice and to complete the table below.

List the Noun Used	List the Noun Job	Singular or Plural	Common or Proper	Simple Subject	Simple Predicate
1.	2.	3.	4.	5.	6.
7.	8.	9.	10.		
11.	12.	13.	14.		

Exercise 3: Name the eight parts of speech that you have studied.

1. _____   2. _____   3. _____   4. _____

5. _____   6. _____   7. _____   8. _____

Exercise 4: Answer each question below on a sheet of notebook paper.

1. List the 8 **be** verbs.
2. What are the parts of a verb phrase?
3. Name the seven subject pronouns.
4. Name the seven possessive pronouns.
5. Name the seven object pronouns.
6. What part of speech is the word NOT?

Exercise 5: Identify each pair of words as synonyms or antonyms by putting parentheses ( ) around **syn** or **ant**.

1. congenial, compatible	syn ant	5. travail, labor	syn ant	9. beseech, entreat	syn ant
2. exuberant, flamboyant	syn ant	6. ancestor, descendant	syn ant	10. lavish, sumptuous	syn ant
3. neutral, partial	syn ant	7. terminate, initiate	syn ant	11. collate, sort	syn ant
4. ambiguous, obvious	syn ant	8. superfluous, redundant	syn ant	12. compulsory, mandatory	syn ant

Exercise 6: Underline the correct homonym in each sentence.

1. I can't wear this (coarse, course) material.
2. (Its, It's) a lovely day for a walk in the park.
3. I need (to, too, two) get my backpack.
4. That is your (forth, fourth) Coke today.
5. The (coarse, course) was hard on the runners.
6. The baby seal swam quickly to (its, it's) mother.
7. The rock cliff is (to, too, two) steep for climbing.
8. Tommy has (to, too, two) new books.

Exercise 7: In your journal, write a paragraph summarizing what you have learned this week.

Chapter 10 Test

Exercise 1: Classify each sentence.

1. _____ A portrait in a ceramic frame sets on Dad's desk in his office.

2. _____ Ouch! My hand hurts in the finger joints!

3. _____ The young boy was sturdily built and could skate extremely fast on the ice.

Exercise 2: Use Sentence 3 to underline the complete subject once and the complete predicate twice and to complete the table below.

List the Noun Used	List the Noun Job	Singular or Plural	Common or Proper	Simple Subject	Simple Predicate
1.	2.	3.	4.	5.	6.
7.	8.	9.	10.		

Exercise 3: Name the eight parts of speech that you have studied.

1. _____ 2. _____ 3. _____ 4. _____

5. _____ 6. _____ 7. _____ 8. _____

Exercise 4: Identify each pair of words as synonyms or antonyms by putting parentheses ( ) around **syn** or **ant**.

1. compulsory, mandatory	syn	ant	5. impulsive, impetuous	syn	ant	9. surmise, guess	syn	ant
2. beseech, entreat	syn	ant	6. permanent, transient	syn	ant	10. superfluous, redundant	syn	ant
3. docile, aggressive	syn	ant	7. neutral, partial	syn	ant	11. terminate, initiate	syn	ant
4. svelte, corpulent	syn	ant	8. edifice, building	syn	ant	12. endorse, denounce	syn	ant

Exercise 5: Underline the correct homonym in each sentence.

1. I love the (sent, scent) that cinnamon has.

2. I will come back with a (knew, new) hair cut.

3. I need to (know, no) where you put my glasses.

4. I (knew, new) in time my dog would come back.

5. Billy (sent, scent) Travis to get the keys for the truck.

6. Tell Karen I said hello when you (right, write) her.

7. I asked my dad for a new motorcycle; he said (know, no).

8. Tommy said he (knew, new) how to diagram a sentence.

Exercise 6: Use the Editing Guide below each sentence to know how many capitalization and punctuation errors to correct. For Sentence 1, write the capitalization and punctuation rule numbers for each correction in bold. For Sentence 2, write the capitalization and punctuation corrections. Use the capitalization and punctuation rule pages to help you.

---

1. **Did Mrs. B**ryant's mother move to **A**thens, **G**reece, on **S**aturday, **M**ay 6, 2001**?**

   Editing Guide: Capitals: 7   Commas: 4   Periods: 1   Apostrophes: 1   End Marks: 1

---

2. dad i believe ill go to andys house to prepare for my english final

   Editing Guide: Capitals: 5   Commas: 1   Apostrophes: 2   End Marks: 1

Exercise 7: In your journal, write a paragraph summarizing what you have learned this week.

Chapter 11 Test A

Exercise 1: <u>Sentence</u>: Write the capitalization and punctuation rule numbers for each correction in bold.

1. **O**ur guide, **Mr. J. M. H**ammond, took us fishing on **C**alico **L**ake near **C**amden, **U**tah.

Editing Guide: Capitals: 9	Commas: 3	Periods: 3	End Marks: 1

Exercise 2: <u>Friendly Letter</u>: Write the capitalization and punctuation corrections only.

500 circle drive

sacramento california 44467

feb 25 20—

dear aunt sara

thank you for the computer you gave dad for christmas its so nice to have a computer around the house i hope youll understand about dads not getting to use it until his turn were having ham for easter see you then

your grateful niece

computer kelly

Editing Guide: Capitals: 20	Commas: 4	Periods: 1	Apostrophes: 4	End Marks: 5

Exercise 3: Name the eight parts of speech that you have studied.

1. _____   2. _____   3. _____   4. _____

5. _____   6. _____   7. _____   8. _____

Exercise 4: Identify each pair of words as synonyms or antonyms by putting parentheses ( ) around **syn** or **ant**.

1. collate, sort	syn ant	5. meager, sparse	syn ant	9. travail, labor	syn ant
2. melancholy, felicitous	syn ant	6. valor, courage	syn ant	10. superfluous, redundant	syn ant
3. swelter, freeze	syn ant	7. permanent, transient	syn ant	11. svelte, corpulent	syn ant
4. edifice, building	syn ant	8. ambiguous, obvious	syn ant	12. pleasurable, tedious	syn ant

Exercise 5: Underline the correct homonym in each sentence.

1. I received (stationary, stationery) in the mail.

2. (Peace, Piece) is what we need all over the world.

3. Jenny (threw, through) her report away.

4. You left (your, you're) books in my car.

5. I would like a large (peace, piece) of your lemon cake.

6. Go (threw, through) the door on your left.

7. A (stationary, stationery) bike is easy to ride.

8. Do you know that (your, you're) late for class?

Exercise 6: In your journal, write a paragraph summarizing what you have learned this week.

Chapter 11 Test B

Exercise 1: Classify each sentence.

1. _____ In a forceful defense, she argued convincingly for her inalienable rights.

2. _____ Stand at the intersection for a closer look at the parade.

3. _____ A sizeable covey of quail suddenly emerged from the overgrown field.

Exercise 2: <u>Sentence</u>: Write the capitalization and punctuation corrections only.

1. i thought of the titanic when tim brad and i boarded our ship for china

Editing Guide: Capitals: 6   Commas: 2   Underline: 1   End Marks: 1

Exercise 3: <u>Friendly Letter</u>: Write the capitalization and punctuation rule numbers for each correction in bold.

300 **S**outh **R**obinson **A**ve.

San **A**ntonio, **T**exas 72023

June 28, 20—

Dear **N**atalie**,**

I broke my leg climbing a tree. **Dr. C**artright, our family doctor**,** put a cast on my leg and told me not to climb trees until **I** get the cast off my leg**. T**his is going to be a dull summer.

I'll go to **V**irginia in **J**une to visit **G**randma. **W**rite soon.

Your cousin**,**

Amy

Editing Guide: Capitals: 21   Commas: 6   Periods: 2   Apostrophes: 1   End Marks: 5

Chapter 12 Test

Exercise 1: Classify each sentence.

1. _____ Homer   tolerates   any   new   medication   very   well.

2. _____ Yesterday, the salamander with the blue tail startled and terrified Jamie's mother.

3. _____ Good grief! The tornado destroyed historical buildings and stately trees

during   its   savage   rampage   across   the   state!

Exercise 2: Use Sentence 3 to underline the complete subject once and the complete predicate twice and to complete the table below.

List the Noun Used	List the Noun Job	Singular or Plural	Common or Proper	Simple Subject	Simple Predicate
1.	2.	3.	4.	5.	6.
7.	8.	9.	10.		
11.	12.	13.	14.		
15.	16.	17.	18.		
19.	20.	21.	22.		

Exercise 3: Identify each pair of words as synonyms or antonyms by putting parentheses ( ) around **syn** or **ant**.

1. impulsive, impetuous	syn ant	5. surmise, guess	syn ant	9. congenial, compatible	syn ant
2. transform, preserve	syn ant	6. permanent, transient	syn ant	10. collate, sort	syn ant
3. compulsory, mandatory	syn ant	7. expedite, hurry	syn ant	11. tactful, undiplomatic	syn ant
4. integrity, honesty	syn ant	8. complicated, intricate	syn ant	12. tawdry, elegant	syn ant

Exercise 4: Underline the correct homonym in each sentence.

1. Your pictures will be ready in one (weak, week).
2. My mother (lead, led) me by my hand.
3. This kitten is so (weak, week) he is not eating.
4. Didn't you (hear, here) me calling you?
5. Plumbers don't like having to use (lead, led) pipes.
6. Come over (hear, here) and read this letter.
7. Nashville is the (capital, capitol) of Tennessee.
8. A sentence always starts with a (capital, capitol) letter.

Exercise 5: For Sentences 1 and 2: Write the capitalization and punctuation corrections only. For Sentence 3: Write the capitalization and punctuation rule numbers for each correction in bold.

1. stan did the german immigrants see hannibal missouri on their way to yosemite national park

Editing Guide: Capitals: 7   Commas: 3   End Marks: 1

2. yes mrs pierce and i went to a very famous italian restaurant called la scala in new york city

Editing Guide: Capitals: 10   Commas: 1   Periods: 1   End Marks: 1

3. **Our** guide, **Ms. B. J. H**arris, took us water skiing at **M**alheur **L**ake near **N**arrows, **O**regon.

Editing Guide: Capitals: 9   Commas: 3   Periods: 3   End Marks: 1

Exercise 6: In your journal, write a paragraph summarizing what you have learned this week.

Chapter 13 Test

Exercise 1: Classify each sentence.

1. _____ After the frost, the farmers quickly harvested the rice crop.

2. _____ Mom and Dad ate a grilled hamburger on the patio in the backyard.

Exercise 2: Use Sentence 2 to underline the complete subject once and the complete predicate twice and to complete the table below.

List the Noun Used	List the Noun Job	Singular or Plural	Common or Proper	Simple Subject	Simple Predicate
1.	2.	3.	4.	5.	6.
7.	8.	9.	10.		
11.	12.	13.	14.		
15.	16.	17.	18.		
19.	20.	21.	22.		

Exercise 3: Identify each pair of words as synonyms or antonyms by putting parentheses ( ) around **syn** or **ant**.

1. meager, sparse	syn ant	5. edifice, building	syn ant	9. impulsive, impetuous	syn ant
2. turbulent, tranquil	syn ant	6. confide, entrust	syn ant	10. obfuscate, confuse	syn ant
3. swelter, freeze	syn ant	7. tawdry, elegant	syn ant	11. profuse, trifling	syn ant
4. pallid, pale	syn ant	8. pleasurable, tedious	syn ant	12. terminate, initiate	syn ant

Exercise 4: Put a slash to separate each run-on sentence below. On notebook paper, correct the run-on sentences by rewriting them as indicated by the labels in parentheses at the end of each sentence.

1. The fish were spawning they were in the shallows. (**CD;**)

2. The seamstress worked at home her husband worked at home. (**SCS**)

3. The children made cookies they ate them for lunch. (**SCV**)

4. The children made cookies they ate them for lunch. (**CD, and**)

5. Jeff installed the generator Larry helped him. (**SCS**)

6. The August heat scalded the tomatoes it also destroyed the pumpkins. (**SCV**)

Exercise 5: Identify each kind of sentence by writing the abbreviation in the blank. (**S, F, SCS, SCV, CD**)

_____ 1. Kale and okra are rich in natural vitamins.

_____ 2. Trash littered the highway, and the scene was unsightly.

_____ 3. Burned down in the middle of the night.

_____ 4. The minister gave the benediction and left the altar.

_____ 5. We must be at the terminal by six; otherwise, we'll miss the train.

_____ 6. The pigeon with the broken wing could not fly.

_____ 7. He seldom complains, yet he suffers excruciating pain.

Exercise 6: Write four sentences using these labels to guide you: (**S**) (**SCS**) (**SCV**) (**CD**)

Exercise 7: In your journal, write a paragraph summarizing what you have learned this week.

Chapter 14 Test

Exercise 1: Classify each sentence.

1. _____ Robert   sent   the   photograph   to   his   friends   in   France   and   Spain.

2. _____ After   twelve   hours   the   jury   acquitted   him   of   the   crime.

Exercise 2: Use Sentence 2 to underline the complete subject once and the complete predicate twice and to complete the table below.

List the Noun Used	List the Noun Job	Singular or Plural	Common or Proper	Simple Subject	Simple Predicate
1.	2.	3.	4.	5.	6.
7.	8.	9.	10.		
11.	12.	13.	14.		

Exercise 3: Identify each pair of words as synonyms or antonyms by putting parentheses ( ) around *syn* or *ant*.

1. integrity, honesty	syn	ant	5. expedite, hurry	syn	ant	9. discourteous, rude	syn	ant
2. svelte, corpulent	syn	ant	6. confide, entrust	syn	ant	10. pallid, pale	syn	ant
3. neutral, partial	syn	ant	7. frigid, torrid	syn	ant	11. superfluous, redundant	syn	ant
4. defunct, extinct	syn	ant	8. triumph, succumb	syn	ant	12. profuse, trifling	syn	ant

Exercise 4: Put a slash to separate each run-on sentence below. On notebook paper, correct the run-on sentences by rewriting them as indicated by the labels in parentheses at the end of each sentence.

1. The   barber   cut   my   hair   he   trimmed   my   mustache. (**SCV**)

2. The   barber   cut   my   hair   he   trimmed   my   mustache. (**CD**;)

3. The   barber   cut   my   hair   he   trimmed   my   mustache. (**CX**, after) (1)

4. The   barber   cut   my   hair   he   trimmed   my   mustache. (**CD**, and)

5. The   barber   trimmed   my   mustache   his   wife   trimmed   my   mustache. (**SCS**)

Exercise 5: Identify each kind of sentence by writing the abbreviation in the blank. (**S, F, SCS, SCV, CD, CX**)

_____ 1. Change your shirt, or I'll not go with you.

_____ 2. I took the class because I needed extra credit.

_____ 3. The actors and actresses spoke compelling lines.

_____ 4. When the wind blows out of the north.

_____ 5. She eats well; nevertheless, she keeps losing weight.

_____ 6 . My son cleaned his room and made his bed before noon today.

_____ 7. Until the ballots are counted, we will not know the winner.

Exercise 6: On notebook paper, write three complex sentences. Underline each subordinate sentence.

Exercise 7: On notebook paper, write five sentences, using these labels to guide you: (**S**) (**SCS**) (**SCV**) (**CD**) (**CX**).

Exercise 8: In your journal, write a paragraph summarizing what you have learned this week.

Chapter 15 Test

Exercise 1: Classify each sentence.

1. _____ My uncle met the mayor of Montpelier during an important business meeting.

2. _____ The strong front did not bring a lot of rain to the barren desert during the night.

Exercise 2: Use Sentence 1 to underline the complete subject once and the complete predicate twice and to complete the table below.

List the Noun Used	List the Noun Job	Singular or Plural	Common or Proper	Simple Subject	Simple Predicate
1.	2.	3.	4.	5.	6.
7.	8.	9.	10.		
11.	12.	13.	14.		
15.	16.	17.	18.		

Exercise 3: Identify each pair of words as synonyms or antonyms by putting parentheses ( ) around **syn** or **ant**.

1. impulsive, impetuous	syn ant	5. confide, entrust	syn ant	9. eccentric, odd	syn ant
2. edifice, building	syn ant	6. profuse, trifling	syn ant	10. aquatic, terrestrial	syn ant
3. transform, preserve	syn ant	7. turbulent, tranquil	syn ant	11. discourteous, rude	syn ant
4. meager, sparse	syn ant	8. discreet, prudent	syn ant	12. mutter, enunciate	syn ant

Exercise 4: Part A: Underline each noun to be made possessive and write singular or plural (**S-P**), the rule number, and the possessive form. Part B: Write each noun as singular possessive and then as plural possessive.

1. For a singular noun - add (**'s**)		2. For a plural noun that ends in **s** - add (**'**)		3. For a plural noun that does not end in **s** - add (**'s**)	
Rule 1: boy's		**Rule 2: boys'**		**Rule 3: men's**	

Part A	S-P	Rule	Possessive Form	Part B	Singular Poss	Plural Poss
1. nurses watches				12. fern		
2. farmer tractor				13. man		
3. dog bowls				14. tornado		
4. monkeys tails				15. secretary		
5. Jan shoe				16. child		
6. agent pen				17. book		
7. Dennis belt				18. wife		
8. puppies paws				19. son		
9. truck tires				20. wolf		
10. Gus money				21. mouse		
11. Jim toothbrush				22. ox		

Exercise 5: On notebook paper, write one sentence for each of these labels: **(S) (SCS) (SCV) (CD) (CX)**.

Exercise 6: In your journal, write a paragraph summarizing what you have learned this week.

Chapter 16 Test

Exercise 1: Classify each sentence.

1. _____ Send your aunt those faded clippings for her scrapbook.

2. _____ The assistant at the public library gave us some helpful suggestions.

3. _____ Did you give Mom and Dad an explanation for your absence?

Exercise 2: Use Sentence 3 to underline the complete subject once and the complete predicate twice and to complete the table below.

List the Noun Used	List the Noun Job	Singular or Plural	Common or Proper	Simple Subject	Simple Predicate
1.	2.	3.	4.	5.	6.
7.	8.	9.	10.		
11.	12.	13.	14.		
15.	16.	17.	18.		

Exercise 3: Identify each pair of words as synonyms or antonyms by putting parentheses ( ) around *syn* or *ant*.

1. compulsory, mandatory	syn ant	5. frigid, torrid	syn ant	9. pallid, pale	syn ant
2. neutral, partial	syn ant	6. triumph, succumb	syn ant	10. ebullient, exhilarated	syn ant
3. valor, courage	syn ant	7. terrestrial, aquatic	syn ant	11. hapless, unlucky	syn ant
4. defunct, extinct	syn ant	8. discreet, prudent	syn ant	12. mutter, enunciate	syn ant

Exercise 4: Underline the correct homonym in each sentence.

1. The (knew, new) library was finished in October.
2. (Their, There, They're) is the dog on the poster.
3. I love the (sent, scent) of your roses.
4. (Their, There, They're) having try-outs for cheerleaders.
5. He (knew, new) the way to Grandma's house.
6. I love the way (their, there, they're) yard is landscaped.

Exercise 5: Identify these pronouns by writing **S** (subjective), **0** (objective), or **P** (possessive) in each blank.
____1. him ____2. I ____3. our ____4. you ____5. she ____6. it ____7. its ____8. us

Exercise 6: For Sentences 1-4, replace each underlined pronoun by writing the correct form in the first blank and **S** or **O** for subjective or objective case in the second blank.

1. Send a card from Lois and <u>I</u>. _____ _____
2. Shirley and <u>me</u> are second cousins._____ _____
3. My aunt and <u>us</u> went fishing today. _____ _____
4. They liked <u>he</u> and <u>I</u>. _____ _____

Exercise 7: Identify each kind of sentence by writing the abbreviation in the blank. (**S, F, SCS, SCV, CD, CX**)

_____ 1. If it doesn't interfere with your schedule.
_____ 2. The telephone and doorbell rang at the same time.
_____ 3. Andrea stood and heaved a sigh of relief.
_____ 4. I wrote one check; however, I must write two more.
_____ 5. Since the flight was cancelled, I had to spend the night at the airport.

Exercise 8: There are three ways to connect compound sentences. Write a sentence demonstrating each one.

Exercise 9: In your journal, write a paragraph summarizing what you have learned this week.

Chapter 17 Test

Exercise 1: Classify each sentence.

1. _____ Send Gloria and Barbara a picture of your hilarious costume.

2. _____ The pilot finally gave the passengers final instructions about their departure.

Exercise 2: Use Sentence 1 to underline the complete subject once and the complete predicate twice and to complete the table below.

List the Noun Used	List the Noun Job	Singular or Plural	Common or Proper	Simple Subject	Simple Predicate
1.	2.	3.	4.	5.	6.
7.	8.	9.	10.		
11.	12.	13.	14.		
15.	16.	17.	18.		

Exercise 3: Identify each pair of words as synonyms or antonyms by putting parentheses ( ) around **syn** or **ant**.

1. appease, antagonize	syn ant	5. expedite, hurry	syn ant	9. impediment, obstacle	syn ant
2. futile, essential	syn ant	6. pleasurable, tedious	syn ant	10. tawdry, elegant	syn ant
3. tactful, undiplomatic	syn ant	7. transform, preserve	syn ant	11. integrity, honesty	syn ant
4. eccentric, odd	syn ant	8. herald, announce	syn ant	12. swelter, freeze	syn ant

Exercise 4: For Sentences 1-4, replace each underlined pronoun by writing the correct form in the first blank and **S** or **O** for subjective or objective case in the second blank.

1. Call Ted and <u>I</u> some evening. _____ _____
2. Teri and <u>me</u> got lost at the mall. _____ _____
3. Dad gave my sister and <u>I</u> a parrot. _____ _____
4. Norman and <u>me</u> were the winners. _____ _____

Exercise 5: Use the Quotation Rules to help punctuate the quotations below. Underline the explanatory words.

1. i thought you knew how to put up a tent snapped ben as sweat rolled into his eyes

2. but ben larry answered i thought you were the one who knew how to put up a tent

3. well i dont ben said as he looked tiredly at the tangled tent and poles

4. larry looked over at his sisters camping spot and said do you want to ask the girls how they got their tent up so fast

Exercise 6: On notebook paper, write one sentence for each of these labels: **(S)** **(SCS)** **(SCV)** **(CD)** **(CX)**.

Exercise 7: On notebook paper, write three sentences, demonstrating each of the three quotations: Beginning quote, end quote, and split quote.

Exercise 8: In your journal, write a paragraph summarizing what you have learned this week.

Chapter 18A Test

Exercise 1: Classify each sentence.

1. _____ Sarah sold Sam and me tables and chairs for our office at home.

2. _____ Will you send me your phone number in Guam?

Exercise 2: Use Sentence 2 to underline the complete subject once and the complete predicate twice and to complete the table below.

List the Noun Used	List the Noun Job	Singular or Plural	Common or Proper	Simple Subject	Simple Predicate
1.	2.	3.	4.	5.	6.
7.	8.	9.	10.		

Exercise 3: Identify each pair of words as synonyms or antonyms by putting parentheses ( ) around *syn* or *ant*.

1. ebullient, exhilarated	syn ant	5. defunct, extinct	syn ant	9. innocuous, harmless	syn ant
2. appease, antagonize	syn ant	6. discreet, prudent	syn ant	10. paraphrased, verbatim	syn ant
3. futile, essential	syn ant	7. constant, variable	syn ant	11. impeccable, flawless	syn ant
4. discourteous, rude	syn ant	8. hapless, unlucky	syn ant	12. felicitous, melancholy	syn ant

Exercise 4: Underline each verb or verb phrase. Identify the verb tense by writing a number **1** for present tense, a number **2** for past tense, and a number **3** for future tense. Write the past tense form and **R** or **I** for Regular or Irregular.

Verb Tense		Main Verb Past Tense Form	R or I
	1. The boys were building a snowman.		
	2. Is he going to school?		
	3. Her pencil was moving rapidly across the page.		
	4. We will be driving to church on Sunday.		
	5. My horse will nibble on your fingers.		
	6. The windows rattled during the blizzard.		
	7. My sister swims everyday.		
	8. We ran after the puppy.		
	9. My parents have gone to church.		
	10. I will be painting the house at noon.		
	11. Were you framing a picture?		
	12. The fireworks will begin at eight o'clock.		

Exercise 5: Identify each kind of sentence by writing the abbreviation in the blank. (**S, F, SCS, SCV, CD, CX**)

_____ 1. The aroma of fried chicken outside the kitchen window.

_____ 2. I cannot go outside until my homework is finished.

_____ 3. The old jalopy coughed and sputtered up the hill.

_____ 4. The trees and shrubs were casualties of the ice storm.

_____ 5. The bridge is closed; however, there is no detour.

Chapter 18B Test

Exercise 6: Change the underlined present tense verbs in Paragraph 1 to past tense verbs in Paragraph 2.

Paragraph 1: Present Tense

My two-year old sister **is** a demolition squad. She **smears** syrup on her pancakes, on the table, and on her hair. Then, she **rolls** the dog s hair, her doll s hair, and her own hair. She **does** not **know** the meaning of nap time. She **cries** until Mom **picks** her up. The rest of the day she **is** grumpy and **gets** into everything. Poor Mom! By supper time, our little demolition squad **sleeps** in her highchair, and no one even **blinks**!

Paragraph 2: Past Tense

My two-year old sister _____ a demolition squad. She _____ syrup on her pancakes, on the table, and on her hair. Then, she _____ the dog's hair, her doll's hair, and her own hair. She _____ not _____ the meaning of nap time. She _____ until Mom _____ her up. The rest of the day she _____ grumpy and _____ into everything. Poor Mom! By supper time, our little demolition squad _____ in her highchair, and no one even _____!

Exercise 7: Change the underlined mixed tense verbs in Paragraph 1 to present tense verbs in Paragraph 2.

Paragraph 1: Mixed Tense

My mom and dad **invited** their best friends to our house for the weekend. They **hadn t seen** their friends for years. They **recruit** me for major cleaning chores. I **kept telling** my mom that I **do** not **understand** all this fuss just because some people **were coming** to visit. I **clean** and **grumbled** all week. As their friends **were getting** out of their car, I **caught** my breath. They **had** a good-looking son, and he **is** just my age! I **raced** into the house and **change** into something more becoming. Then, I quickly **checked** my hair again. Mom **said** that she **did** not **understand** all this fuss just because a boy **comes** to visit.

Paragraph 2: Present Tense

My mom and dad _____ their best friends to our house for the weekend. They _____ _____ their friends for years. They _____ me for major cleaning chores. I _____ _____ my mom that I _____ not _____ all this fuss just because some people _____ _____ to visit. I _____ and _____ all week. As their friends _____ _____ out of their car, I _____ my breath. They _____ a good-looking son, and he _____ just my age! I _____ into the house and _____ into something more becoming. Then, I quickly _____ my hair again. Mom _____ that she _____ not _____ all the fuss just because a boy _____ to visit.

Exercise 8: On notebook paper, write one sentence for each of these labels: **(S) (SCS) (SCV) (CD) (CX)**.

Exercise 9: On notebook paper, write the seven present tense helping verbs, the five past tense helping verbs, and the two future tense helping verbs.

Exercise 10: In your journal, write a paragraph summarizing what you have learned this week.

Chapter 19 Test

Exercise 1: Classify each sentence.

1. _____ The bride is a beautiful, friendly, fun-loving member of a professional family.

2. _____ Sam was a master at golf during his adolescence.

3. _____ The moon is a very necessary heavenly body.

Exercise 2: Identify each pair of words as synonyms or antonyms by putting parentheses ( ) around *syn* or *ant*.

1. herald, announce	syn ant	5. eccentric, odd	syn ant	9. frigid, torrid	syn ant
2. vindicate, indict	syn ant	6. unappealing, winsome	syn ant	10. tranquil, turbulent	syn ant
3. volunteer, coerce	syn ant	7. sensitive, callous	syn ant	11. surmise, guess	syn ant
4. terrestrial, aquatic	syn ant	8. impeccable, flawless	syn ant	12. tactful, undiplomatic	syn ant

Exercise 3: Change the underlined mixed tense verbs in Paragraph 1 to past tense verbs in Paragraph 2.

Paragraph 1: Mixed Tenses

Blinky **was** my beloved computer. He **helps** me when I **check** my homework. I **am** tired tonight, so I **program** Blinky to work my math problems. When my mom **looks** over them, she **told** me all my problems **are** wrong! My mouth **dropped** open. I **march** back into my room and **glare** at Blinky. I **tapped** my fingers angrily beside Blinky's keyboard. I finally **decide** to check Blinky's command system. Then, I **groan** loudly. It **isn't** Blinky's fault after all. It **is** Dad's fault. He **had programmed** Blinky not to do my homework.

Paragraph 2: Past Tense

Blinky _____ my beloved computer. He _____ me when I _____ my homework. I _____ tired tonight, so I _____ Blinky to work my math problems. When my mom _____ over them, she _____ me all my problems _____ wrong! My mouth _____ open. I _____ back into my room and _____ at Blinky. I _____ my fingers angrily beside Blinky's keyboard. I finally _____ to check Blinky's command system. Then, I _____ loudly. It _____ Blinky's fault after all. It _____ Dad's fault. He _____ _____ Blinky not to do my homework.

Exercise 4: Copy the following words on notebook paper. Write the correct contraction beside each word.
Words: you have, there is, is not, you are, they will, will not, it is, he will, let us, we would, I will, you will, was not, do not, they have, I am, does not, have not.

Exercise 5: Copy the following contractions on notebook paper. Write the correct words beside each contraction.
Contractions: they're, he's, you're, hasn't, you'd, we've, doesn't, hadn't, can't, I'd, don't.

Exercise 6: Write the seven present tense helping verbs, the five past tense helping verbs, and the two future tense helping verbs.

Exercise 7: In your journal, write a paragraph summarizing what you have learned this week.

Chapter 20 Test

Exercise 1: Classify each sentence.

1. _____ My brother's first three cars were antiques.

2. _____ During the fire, the ushers became heroes in the eyes of the panicked victims.

Exercise 2: Identify each pair of words as synonyms or antonyms by putting parentheses ( ) around **syn** or **ant**.

1. constant, variable	syn ant	4. brazen, decent	syn ant	7. malleable, pliable	syn ant
2. free, liberate	syn ant	5. brevity, longevity	syn ant	8. manifold, numerous	syn ant
3. paraphrased, verbatim	syn ant	6. ludicrous, ridiculous	syn ant	9. appease, antagonize	syn ant

Exercise 3: Underline the negative words in each sentence. Rewrite each sentence and correct the double negative mistake as indicated by the rule number in parentheses at the end of the sentence.

Rule 1	Rule 2	Rule 3
Change the second negative to a positive.	Take out the negative part of a contraction.	Remove the first negative word (verb change).

1. She didn't hear no sirens approaching. (Rule 1)

2. He wouldn't never distort the truth. (Rule 2)

3. They couldn't see nothing in the dark. (Rule 1)

4. I didn't see nothing in the closet. (Rule 3)

5. Arthur didn't never require assistance. (Rule 3)

6. I won't ask nothing about it. (Rule 1)

7. There isn't no room for error. (Rule 1)

8. Keith couldn't find no cuff links. (Rule 2)

Exercise 4: Write the rule numbers and the different forms for the adjectives below. For irregular forms, write **Irr**.

Comparative: Rule 1: Use **-er** with 1 or 2 syllable words and **more** with -ful words, awkward words, or words with 3 or more syllables.
Superlative: Rule 2: Use **-est** with 1 or 2 syllable words and **most** with -ful words, awkward words, or words with 3 or more syllables.

Simple Adjective Form	Rule Box	Comparative Adjective Form	Rule Box	Superlative Adjective Form
1. supportive				
2. cute				
3. well				
4. restless				
5. ill				
6. talkative				
7. deadly				

Exercise 5: In each blank, write the correct form of the adjective in parentheses to complete the sentences.

1. The algebra problem was the _____ part of the test. (complex)

2. The little girl's hair was _____ than her mother's hair. (short)

3. Ms. Jones was a very _____ tutor in junior high. (nice)

4. Chocolate ice cream is _____ than frozen yogurt. (good)

Exercise 6: In your journal, write a paragraph summarizing what you have learned this week.

Chapter 21 Test

Exercise 1: Classify each sentence.

1. _____ My grandmother's ancient fur coat is a conversation piece.

2. _____ The saddle and bridle are essential parts of equestrian equipment.

Exercise 2: Identify each pair of words as synonyms or antonyms by putting parentheses ( ) around *syn* or *ant*.

1. unappealing, winsome	syn ant	4. brevity, longevity	syn ant	7. monstrous, enormous	syn ant
2. sensitive, callous	syn ant	5. manifold, numerous	syn ant	8. ludicrous, ridiculous	syn ant
3. malleable, pliable	syn ant	6. mendicant, beggar	syn ant	9. predictable, capricious	syn ant

Exercise 3: Parts 1 and 2: Choose an answer from the choices in parentheses. Fill in the other columns according to the titles. (**S** or **P** stands for singular or plural. **N/Pro** means to identify the subject as a noun or pronoun.)

Part 1: Pronoun-antecedent agreement

	Pronoun Choice	S or P	Antecedent	S or P
1. The flags on the street have lost (its, their) luster.				
2. His campaign for tax reform had lost (its, their) intensity.				
3. The missionaries in Egypt have lost (his, their) citizenship.				
4. Nobody in Paris dislikes (his, their) city.				

Part 2: Subject-verb Agreement

	Subject	N/Pro	S or P	Verb choice
5. Each of the pillars (is, are) leaning.				
6. Both of the dorms (seem, seems) deserted.				
7. The front tires on the truck (is, are) deflated.				
8. The road to happiness (is, are) paved with hurdles.				

Part 3: Identify the indefinite pronouns as singular (S), plural (P), or either (E) singular or plural.

____ 1. everyone ____ 2. few ____ 3. anybody ____ 4. another ____ 5. all

Part 4: On notebook paper, write these indefinite pronouns: 17 singular indefinite pronouns (4/one, 4/body, 3/thing, 6/one or none), 5 plural indefinite pronouns, and 6 singular/plural indefinite pronouns.

Exercise 4: Underline the negative words in each sentence. Rewrite each sentence and correct the double negative mistake as indicated by the rule number in parentheses at the end of the sentence.

Rule 1	Rule 2	Rule 3
Change the second negative to a positive.	Take out the negative part of a contraction.	Remove the first negative word (verb change).

1. She didn't ask no questions today. (Rule 3)

3. She wasn't never early. (Rule 2)

_____

2. She doesn't never wear a jacket. (Rule 3)

4. He didn't get no rest last night. (Rule 1)

_____

Exercise 5: On notebook paper, write three sentences, demonstrating each of the three degrees of adjectives. Identify the form you used by writing **simple, comparative, or superlative** at the end of each sentence.

Exercise 6: On notebook paper, write three sentences in which you demonstrate each of the double negative rules. Underline the negative word in each sentence.

Exercise 7: In your journal, write a paragraph summarizing what you have learned this week.

Chapter 22 Test

Exercise 1: Classify each sentence.

1. _____ Those bats in the cave are quite scary.

2. _____ The alligator in the swamp is dirty and mean.

3. _____ The traffic on the expressway is heavy in the mornings.

Exercise 2: Use Sentence 3 to underline the complete subject once and the complete predicate twice and to complete the table below.

List the Noun Used	List the Noun Job	Singular or Plural	Common or Proper	Simple Subject	Simple Predicate
1.	2.	3.	4.	5.	6.
7.	8.	9.	10.		
11.	12.	13.	14.		

Exercise 3: Identify each pair of words as synonyms or antonyms by putting parentheses ( ) around **syn** or **ant**.

1. verbose, prolix	syn ant	6. herald, announce	syn ant	11. mendicant, beggar	syn ant
2. futile, essential	syn ant	7. volunteer, coerce	syn ant	12. chastise, applaud	syn ant
3. constant, variable	syn ant	8. clarify, obscure	syn ant	13. impeccable, flawless	syn ant
4. vindicate, indict	syn ant	9. predictable, capricious	syn ant	14. malleable, pliable	syn ant
5. nebulous, vague	syn ant	10. remiss, negligent	syn ant	15. paraphrased, verbatim	syn ant

Exercise 4: Write rule number from Reference 68 and the correct plural form of the nouns below.

	Rule	Plural Form			Rule	Plural Form
1. alley				11. box		
2. calf				12. radio		
3. roof				13. tomato		
4. deer				14. cat		
5. child				15. try		
6. turkey				16. fox		
7. pony				17. goose		
8. mouse				18. sheep		
9. rodeo				19. church		
10. half				20. sheriff		

Exercise 5: Write the seven present tense helping verbs, the five past tense helping verbs, and the two future tense helping verbs.

Exercise 6: On notebook paper, make a list of twelve contractions, then write the words from which the contractions come.

Exercise 7: On notebook paper, write one sentence for each of these labels: **(S) (SCS) (SCV) (CD) (CX)**.

Exercise 8: On notebook paper, write three sentences, demonstrating each of the three quotations. Underline the explanatory words.

Exercise 9: In your journal, write a paragraph summarizing what you have learned this week.

Chapter 23 Test

Exercise 1: Classify each sentence.

1. _____ My aunt was nervous about her surgery today.

2. _____ The president's responsibility to the class was very obvious.

Exercise 2: Identify each pair of words as synonyms or antonyms by putting parentheses ( ) around **syn** or **ant**.

1. comply, resist	syn ant	4. brevity, longevity	syn ant	7. innocuous, harmless	syn ant
2. disparate, uniform	syn ant	5. oppressive, overbearing	syn ant	8. impediment, obstacle	syn ant
3. revolting, disgusting	syn ant	6. clarify, obscure	syn ant	9. volunteer, coerce	syn ant

Exercise 3: For Parts 1 and 2, choose an answer from the choices in parentheses. Then, fill in the rest of the columns according to the titles. (**S** or **P** stands for singular or plural. **N/Pro** means to identify the subject as a noun or pronoun.)

Part 1: Pronoun-antecedent agreement

	Pronoun Choice	S or P	Antecedent	S or P
1. The geese on the lake are shedding (its, their) feathers.				
2. The old man in the park has lost (his, their) teeth.				
3. Everything on the table is in (its, their) place.				
4. My shoes have lost (its, their) soles.				

Part 2: Subject-verb Agreement

	Subject	N/Pro	S or P	Verb choice
5. Many tornadoes (was, were) popping out of the sky.				
6. The paintings in the foyer (is, are) classics.				
7. Somebody in the room (is, are) snoring.				
8. One of the maps (is, are) torn.				

Exercise 4: Write the seven present tense helping verbs, the five past tense helping verbs, and the two future tense helping verbs.

Exercise 5: On notebook paper, write these indefinite pronouns: 17 singular indefinite pronouns (4/one, 4/body, 3/thing, 6/one or none), 5 plural indefinite pronouns, and 6 singular/plural indefinite pronouns.

Exercise 6: On notebook paper, write three sentences, demonstrating each of the three degrees of adjectives. Identify the form you used by writing **simple, comparative, or superlative** at the end of each sentence.

Exercise 7: On notebook paper, identify the parts of a friendly letter and envelope by writing the titles and an example for each title.

Exercise 8: On notebook paper, write one sentence for each of these labels: **(S) (SCS) (SCV) (CD) (CX)**.

Exercise 9: On notebook paper, write three sentences in which you demonstrate each of the double negative rules. Underline the negative word in each sentence. (Use your book for the double negative rules.)

Exercise 10: In your journal, write a paragraph summarizing what you have learned this week.

Chapter 24 Test

Exercise 1: Classify each sentence.

1. _____ The lettering on our mailbox is crooked and illegible.

2. _____ Kelly's crops were exceptionally green for a beginning gardener.

Exercise 2: Identify each pair of words as synonyms or antonyms by putting parentheses ( ) around *syn* or *ant*.

1. predictable, capricious	syn ant	4. chastise, applaud	syn ant	7. paltry, insignificant	syn ant
2. brazen, decent	syn ant	5. perjury, untruth	syn ant	8. revolting, disgusting	syn ant
3. manifold, numerous	syn ant	6. comply, resist	syn ant	9. manageable, incorrigible	syn ant

Exercise 3: On notebook paper, identify the parts of a business letter and envelope by writing the titles and an example for each title.

Exercise 4: Write the seven present tense helping verbs, the five past tense helping verbs, and the two future tense helping verbs.

Exercise 5: On notebook paper, write these indefinite pronouns: 17 singular indefinite pronouns (4/one, 4/body, 3/thing, 6/one or none), 5 plural indefinite pronouns, and 6 singular/plural indefinite pronouns.

Exercise 6: On notebook paper, write three sentences, demonstrating each of the three degrees of adjectives. Identify the form you used by writing **simple, comparative, or superlative** at the end of each sentence.

Exercise 7: On notebook paper, identify the parts of a friendly letter and envelope by writing the titles and an example for each title.

Exercise 8: On notebook paper, write one sentence for each of these labels: **(S) (SCS) (SCV) (CD) (CX)**.

Exercise 9: On notebook paper, write three sentences in which you demonstrate each of the double negative rules. Underline the negative word in each sentence. (Use your book for the double negative rules.)

Exercise 10: In your journal, write a paragraph summarizing what you have learned this week.

Chapter 25 Test

Exercise 1: Classify each sentence.

1. _____ Pollutants and erosion are the worst enemies of rivers.

2. _____ The mayor is elected by the residents and serves for two years.

3. _____ The research gave us a cure for our condition!

Exercise 2: Identify each pair of words as synonyms or antonyms by putting parentheses ( ) around **syn** or **ant**.					
1. authentic, counterfeit	syn ant	4. verbose, prolix	syn ant	7. pious, sacred	syn ant
2. pilfer, steal	syn ant	5. monstrous, enormous	syn ant	8. barbaric, civilized	syn ant
3. sensitive, callous	syn ant	6. deify, vilify	syn ant	9. paltry, insignificant	syn ant

Exercise 3: Write another thank-you note. First, think of a person who has done something nice for you or has given you a gift (*even the gift of time*). Next, write that person a thank-you note, using the information in the Reference section as a guide.

Exercise 4: Make another invitation card. First, think of a special event or occasion and who will be invited. Next, make an invitation to send out, using the information in the Reference section as a guide. Illustrate your card appropriately.

Exercise 5: Write the seven present tense helping verbs, the five past tense helping verbs, and the two future tense helping verbs.

Exercise 6: On notebook paper, write these indefinite pronouns: 17 singular indefinite pronouns (4/one, 4/body, 3/thing, 6/one or none), 5 plural indefinite pronouns, and 6 singular/plural indefinite pronouns.

Exercise 7: On notebook paper, write three sentences, demonstrating each of the three degrees of adjectives. Identify the form you used by writing **simple, comparative, or superlative** at the end of each sentence.

Exercise 8: On notebook paper, identify the parts of a friendly letter and envelope by writing the titles and an example for each title.

Exercise 9: On notebook paper, write one sentence for each of these labels: **(S) (SCS) (SCV) (CD) (CX)**.

Exercise 10: On notebook paper, write three sentences in which you demonstrate each of the double negative rules. Underline the negative word in each sentence. (Use your book for the double negative rules.)

Exercise 11: In your journal, write a paragraph summarizing what you have learned this week.

Chapter 26 Test

Exercise 1: Classify each sentence.

1. _____ Car   salesmen   can   exaggerate   the   truth.

2. _____ Numerous   doctors   have   given   the   hospital   good   reviews.

3. _____ The   frogs   and   snakes   patiently   waited   on   the   rotten   logs.

Exercise 2: Identify each pair of words as synonyms or antonyms by putting parentheses ( ) around **syn** or **ant**.

1. vindicate, indict	syn ant	5. recant, withdraw	syn ant	9. pilfer, steal	syn ant
2. volunteer, coerce	syn ant	6. intensify, placate	syn ant	10. pious, sacred	syn ant
3. ebullient, exhilarated	syn ant	7. disparate, uniform	syn ant	11. oppressive, overbearing	syn ant
4. innocuous, harmless	syn ant	8. recline, repose	syn ant	12. requirement, option	syn ant

Exercise 3: Match each part of a book listed below with the type of information it may give you. Write the appropriate letter in the blank. You may use each letter only once.

A. Title Page	B. Copyright Page	C. Index	D. Bibliography	E. Appendix	F. Glossary

1. _____ A list of books used by the author as references   4. _____ ISBN number

2. _____ Meanings of important words in the book   5. _____ Used to locate topics quickly

3. _____ Publisher's name and city where the book was published   6. _____ Extra maps in a book

Exercise 4: Match each part of a book listed below with the type of information it may give you. Write the appropriate letter in the blank. You may use each letter only once.

A. Title Page   B. Table of Contents   C. Copyright Page   D. Index   E. Bibliography
F. Preface   G. Body

1. _____ Exact page numbers for a particular topic   4. _____ Text of the book

2. _____ Author's name, title of book, and illustrator s name   5. _____ Reason the book was written

3. _____ Books listed for finding more information   6. _____ Titles of units and chapters

7. _____ Copyright date

Exercise 5: Write the five parts found at the front of a book.

Exercise 6: Write the four parts found at the back of a book.

Exercise 7: In your journal, write a paragraph summarizing what you have learned this week.

Chapter 27A Test

Exercise 1: Classify each sentence.

1. _____ People watched the fireworks on the floodwall of the town.

2. _____ Darrin's cousin was the winner of the race.

3. _____ Are you going to the barbecue tonight?

Exercise 2: Identify each pair of words as synonyms or antonyms by putting parentheses ( ) around **syn** or **ant**.

1. nebulous, vague	syn ant	4. manageable, incorrigible	syn ant	7. succinct, brief	syn ant
2. obstreperous, rambunctious	syn ant	5. subvert, undermine	syn ant	8. intensify, placate	syn ant
3. routine, systematic	syn ant	6. authentic, counterfeit	syn ant	9. recline, repose	syn ant

Exercise 3: Use the Table of Contents example in Reference 79 to answer the following questions on another sheet of paper.

1. Look over the chapter titles. What is this book about?

2. How many chapters are in this book?

3. What is the last page number of Chapter 6?

4. Your mom has finally agreed to let you have a dog! You have to decide what kind of dog would do best in your apartment. What chapter would you use to help you solve your problems?

5. Dad says your bulldog, Fido, needs to learn to fetch the newspaper. You don't know how to teach him. What chapter will help you? Beginning Page?

6. What is the title of the chapter that will give you some advice about what to do with a "senior citizen" collie?

7. Your basset hound, Bullet, loves to eat. His little legs can hardly keep his fat tummy off the ground. Write the numbers of two chapters that can help you trim the weight off Bullet.

8. You have a ferocious poodle named Killer. Find out how often he needs a rabies shot. On what page would you begin looking?

9. You named your German shepherd puppy Peaches that you received as a birthday present. Write the title of the chapter that tells you how to take care of her.

10. Your cocker spaniel needs a haircut and has fleas. What is the number of the chapter that tells how often you can treat your dog for fleas?

11. **Bonus**: How many pages are in Chapter 5?

Exercise 4: Answer the following questions about an index on another sheet of paper.

1. What are three main reasons to use an index?
2. Where is an index located?
3. How does an index list information?
4. When an index lists key ideas in a book, what are the key ideas called?
5. When an index lists specific information under the topic, what is it called?
6. What do the numbers following topics and subtopics tell?

Chapter 27B Test

Exercise 5: Underline the correct answer for numbers 1-6. Write the correct answers for numbers 7-8.

1. Nonfiction books are arranged on the shelves by (**numerical order   alphabetical order**).
2. Biographies and autobiographies are arranged by (**numerical order   alphabetical order**).
3. Fiction books are arranged on the shelves by (**numerical order   alphabetical order**).
4. The main reference book that is primarily a book of maps is the
   (**encyclopedia   dictionary   atlas   almanac**).
5. The main reference book that gives the definition, spelling, and pronunciation of words is the
   (**encyclopedia   dictionary   atlas   almanac**).
6. The main reference book that is published once a year with a variety of up-to-date information is the
   (**encyclopedia   dictionary   atlas   almanac**).
7. What would you find by going to *The Readers' Guide to Periodical Literature*? _____
8. What are the names of the three types of cards located in the card catalog? _____

Exercise 6: Put the fiction books below in the correct order to go on the shelves. Write numbers 1-7 in the blanks to show the correct order.

1. *Trouble River* by Betsy Byars   _____
2. *No Place for Love* by Joan Lingard   _____
3. *Prince Caspian* by C.S. Lewis   _____
4. *The Shy Ones* by Lynn Hall   _____
5. *A Wrinkle in Time* by Madeleine L'Engle   _____
6. *The Survivor* by Robb White   _____
7. *Follow My Leader* by James B. Garfield   _____

Exercise 7: Write True or False for each statement.

1. Fiction and nonfiction books have numbers on their spines to locate them on a shelf. _____
2. The title of the book is always the first line on each of the catalog cards. _____
3. The books in the fiction section are arranged alphabetically by the author's last name. _____
4. The *Readers' Guide to Periodical Literature* is an index to magazines. _____
5. Biographies are arranged on the shelves according to the author's last name. _____
6. Encyclopedias give concise information about persons, places, and events of world-wide interest. _____
7. The card catalog is an index to books in the library. _____
8. The books in the nonfiction section are arranged numerically by a call number. _____

Exercise 8: Draw and label the three catalog cards for this book on a sheet of notebook paper: 213.6 *The Art of Modern Music* by Stephanie Lambert, Braxton City Press, Dallas, 1999, 254 p. *(Use the catalog card examples in Reference 77.)*

Exercise 9: In your journal, write a paragraph summarizing what you have learned this week.

Chapter 28 Test

Exercise 1: Classify each sentence.

1. _____ Several   scouts   were   frantically   searching   for   Ed   and   me.

2. _____ Sixteen Asian artists painted a morning scene on the concrete floodwall.

3. _____ Will   you   give   us   special   permission   at   noon   tomorrow?

Exercise 2: Identify each pair of words as synonyms or antonyms by putting parentheses ( ) around *syn* or *ant*.

1. deify, vilify	syn ant	7. periodic, systematic	syn ant	13. mutter, enunciate	syn ant
2. requirement, option	syn ant	8. obstreperous, rambunctious	syn ant	14. free, liberate	syn ant
3. perjury, untruth	syn ant	9. serene, tranquil	syn ant	15. endorse, denounce	syn ant
4. ameliorate, deteriorate	syn ant	10. barbaric, civilized	syn ant	16. pious, sacred	syn ant
5. prosperity, adversity	syn ant	11. taint, contaminate	syn ant	17. succinct, brief	syn ant
6. subvert, undermine	syn ant	12. chastise, applaud	syn ant	18. brazen, decent	syn ant

Exercise 3: Copy the notes below into a two-point outline. Change wording to put notes into correct parallel form.

Notes	Outline
seasonal migration	
spring migration	
waterways	
the last freeze	
migration in the fall	
after harvest	
preceding killing frost	

Exercise 4: On notebook paper, write all the jingles that you can recall from memory. There is a total of 21 jingles. Tell which jingle you liked best and why.

Exercise 5: In your journal, write a paragraph summarizing what you have learned this week.

SHURLEY ENGLISH ABBREVIATIONS FOR LEVEL 6

Abbreviation	Description
N	Noun
SN	Subject Noun
CSN	Compound Subject Noun
Pro	Pronoun
SP	Subject Pronoun
CSP	Compound Subject Pronoun
V	Verb
HV	Helping Verb
CV	Compound Verb
V-t	Verb-transitive
CV-t	Compound Verb-transitive
LV	Linking Verb
CLV	Compound Linking Verb
A	Article Adjective
Adj	Adjective
CAdj	Compound Adjective
Adv	Adverb
CAdv	Compound Adverb
P	Preposition
OP	Object of the Preposition
COP	Compound Object of the Preposition

	Description
PPA	Possessive Pronoun Adjective
PNA	Possessive Noun Adjective
C	Conjunction
I	Interjection
DO	Direct Object
CDO	Compound Direct Object
IO	Indirect Object
CIO	Compound Indirect Object
PrN	Predicate Noun
PrP	Predicate Pronoun
CPrN	Compound Predicate Noun
CPrP	Compound Predicate Pronoun
PA	Predicate Adjective
CPA	Compound Predicate Adjective

	Sentences
D	Declarative Sentence
E	Exclamatory Sentence
Int	Interrogative Sentence
Imp	Imperative Sentence

	Level 6 Patterns
SN V P1	Subject Noun Verb Pattern 1
SN V-t DO P2	Subject Noun Verb-transitive Direct Object Pattern 2
SN V-t IO DO P3	Subject Noun Verb-transitive Indirect Object Direct Object Pattern 3
SN LV PrN P4	Subject Noun Linking Verb Predicate Noun Pattern 4
SN LV PA P5	Subject Noun Linking Verb Predicate Adjective Pattern 5